lonely planet

# POCKET

# VIENNA

TOP EXPERIENCES • LOCAL LIFE

W0387242

CATHERINE LE NEVEZ, KERRY WALKER, MARC DI DUCA

# Contents



Prater (p132)
LIPSKIY/SHUTTERSTOCK ©

## Explore Vienna 35



## Survival Guide 143



## COVID-19

We have re-checked every business in this book before publication to ensure that it is still open after the COVID-19 outbreak. However, the economic and social impacts of COVID-19 will continue to be felt long after the outbreak has been contained, and many businesses, services and events referenced in this guide may experience ongoing restrictions. Some businesses may be temporarily closed, have changed their opening hours and services, or require bookings; some unfortunately could have closed permanently. We suggest you check with venues before visiting for the latest information.

## Special Features

# Top Experiences

## Revisit the Past at Kunsthistorisches Museum Vienna

Vienna's richest treasure chest. p74

ROSSHELEN/SHUTTERSTOCK ©

S4SVISUALS/SHUTTERSTOCK ©

## Lord it Up at Royal Hofburg

Six-and-a-half centuries of imperial history. **p38**

## Raise the Curtain on the Staatsoper

World-renowned opera and ballet venue. **p98**

POSZTOS/SHUTTERSTOCK ©

S.BORISOV/SHUTTERSTOCK ©

## Marvel at Stephansdom

Vienna's Gothic wonder. **p56**

## Stroll in Schloss Belvedere & Gardens

Vienna's most sublime baroque palace. **p114**

HELEN CATHCART/LONELY PLANET ©

TASFOTONL/GETTY IMAGES © MUMOK ARCHITECTS: ORTNER & ORTNER

## Explore Past and Present at MuseumsQuartier

Imperial stables turned museum ensemble. **p80**

## Time Hop at Naturhistorisches Museum

Minerals, fossils and dinosaur bones. **p84**

S4SVISUALS/SHUTTERSTOCK ©

MARTIN HOLLAUS/500PX ©

## Channel Mozart at Schloss Schönbrunn & Gardens

Sun-yellow palace. **p136**

## Run Wild at Prater

Park life and funfair thrills. **p132**

SOO HON KEONG/GETTY IMAGES ©

# Dining Out

*Dining in Vienna gives you a taste of the city's history, at its street stands sizzling up sausages, candlelit vaulted-cellar wine bars and earthy, wood-panelled* Beisln *(bistro pubs); its present, at hip cafes, multiethnic markets and international eateries; and its future, at innovative spaces with a wave of exciting chefs pushing in new directions.*

## Local Specialities

**Schnitzel** *Wiener Schnitzel* (Viennese cutlet; pictured) should always be crumbed veal, but pork is gaining ground.

**Goulash** *Rindsgulasch* (beef goulash) is everywhere in Vienna.

**Tafelspitz** Traditionally this boiled prime beef swims in the juices of locally produced *Suppengrün* (fresh soup vegetables), before being served with *Kren* (horseradish) sauce.

**Beuschel** Offal, usually sliced lung and heart with a slightly creamy sauce.

**Backhendl** Fried, breaded chicken, often called *steirischer Backhendl* (Styrian fried chicken).

**Apfelstrudel** Apple strudel.

**Zwiebelrostbraten** Slices of roast beef smothered in gravy and fried onions.

**Schinkenfleckerln** Oven-baked ham-and-noodle casserole.

**Bauernschmaus** Platter of cold meats.

**Kaiserschmarrn** Sweet pancake with raisins.

**Marillenknödel** Apricot dumplings; served in summer.

## Prices

Prices refer to a two-course meal, excluding drinks:

**€** under €15
**€€** €15-€30
**€€€** over €30

## Best Dining Experiences

**Steirereck im Stadtpark** Vienna's class act by the Wien River. (p126)

**Lingenhel** Deli-shop-bar-restaurant in a 200-year-old house. (p128)

**Plachutta** The ultimate place for Viennese *Tafelspitz*. (p61)

**Griechenbeisl** The history-soaked *Beisl* of your dreams. (p67)

**Meinl's Restaurant** Exceptional quality through the seasons, with an on-site wine bar and providore. (p48)

## Best Goulash

**Meierei im Stadtpark** Some speak of the world's best. (p127)

STEPANEK PHOTOGRAPHY/SHUTTERSTOCK ©

**Glacis Beisl** Authentic goulash in the Museums-Quartier. (p92)

## Best Snacks

**Bitzinger Würstelstand am Albertinaplatz** Iconic sausage stand opposite the opera. (p47)

**Naschmarkt** Market stalls and sit-down eateries galore. (p111)

**Trzesniewski** Upmarket open-faced sandwiches. (p48)

## Best Schnitzels

**Figlmüller** Bills itself as the home of the *Schnitzel*. (p57)

**Huth Gastwirtschaft** Neo-*Beisl* that serves a superb *Wiener Schnitzel*. (p66)

## Best Vegetarian & Vegan

**Tian** Michelin-starred vegetarian cuisine. (p66)

**Swing Kitchen** Sensational vegan burgers. (p92)

**Vegiezz** Bright, white cafe with all-vegan fare. (p107)

## Worth a Trip

Shimmering in gunmetal grey, with floor-to-ceiling windows, **Das Loft** (01-90 616 8110; www.dasloftwien.at; 02, Praterstrasse 1; meals €22-39; 6.30-10.30am Mon-Fri, to 11am Sat & Sun, 12.30-2.30pm & 6-11pm daily; P; U Schwedenplatz) has uninterrupted views across the city skyline on the Danube Canal. Perch on leather swivel chairs over brunch or cocktails and peer down upon Prater Park and Stefansdom. Dinner menus offer up to five courses of 'fusion' cuisine.

# Vienna on a Plate

## Sacher Torte

A tangy layer of apricot jam cuts through the sweetness.

A chocolate seal displays the torte's creator.

Rich, glossy chocolate icing covers the torte.

Unsweetened *Schlagobers* (whipped cream) makes the perfect accompaniment.

Vienna's famous *Sacher Torte* is made from a chocolate sponge.

KEMTER/GETTY IMAGES ©

## ★ Top Five for Sacher Torte

**Café Sacher** (p51)

**Demel** (p51)

**Café Mozart** (p48)

**Café Schwarzenberg** (p108)

**Café Sperl** (p107)

## Sacher Torte in Vienna

Franz Sacher created the *Sacher Torte* in 1832 for Prince Klemens Wenzel von Metternich. Sacher's son, Eduard, brought the original recipe and sole distribution rights to Demel in 1934. Until 1963 legal battles raged between Demel and Café Sacher over the trade-mark and title. An out-of-court settlement gave Café Sacher the rights to the phrase 'Original Sacher Torte', and Demel to use a decorative triangular seal reading 'Eduard-Sacher-Torte'.

Café Sperl (p107)

MOJMIR FOTOGRAFIE/SHUTTERSTOCK ©

# Bar Open

*In this city, where history often waltzes with the cutting edge, the drinking scene spans 18th-century vaulted wine cellars to boisterous beer gardens, boho student dives, and cocktail, retro and rooftop bars. And, with over 700 hectares of vineyards within city limits, a visit to a* Heuriger *(wine tavern) is a quintessential Viennese experience.*

KRZYSZTOF DYDYNSKI/LONELY PLANET ©

## Grape & Grain

While wine is the chosen drink of the Viennese, beer also features heavily in the city's cultural make-up. Try the following:

**Blauburgunder** Complex, fruity Pinot Noir red.

**Grüner Veltliner** Strong, fresh white wine with hints of citrus and pear.

**Riesling** Fruity white wine with strong acidity.

**Zweigelt** Full-bodied red wine with intense cherry aromas.

**Dunkel** Thick dark beer with a very rich flavour.

**Helles** Lager with a bite – clear and lightly hoppy.

**Pils** Crisp, strong and often bitter Pilsner beer.

**Märzen** Red-coloured beer with a strong malt taste.

**Zwickel** Unfiltered beer with a cloudy complexion.

**Schnäpse** (schnapps) Fruit brandy; usually consumed after a meal.

## Useful Websites

**Falter** (www.falter.at) Event and party listings.

**Vienna Online** (www.vienna.at) Keep track of club nights with this event calendar.

**Tourist Info Wien** (www.wien.info) Nightlife listings arranged by theme.

## Prices

Standard beer prices range from €2 to €5, depending on the venue and location (central Vienna tends to be more expensive). A decent glass of local wine starts at around €2. Expect to pay at least €7 for a simple mixed drink and around €9 and up for a cocktail.

## Best Wine Bars

**Vinothek W-Einkehr** Superb Austrian wines. (p61)

**Sekt Comptoir** Effervescent bar with Burgenland *Sekt* (sparkling wine) near the Naschmarkt. (p101)

**Esterházykeller** Serves wines from the Esterházy Palace wine estate. (p51)

**Villon** Set deep below ground in a 500-year-old cellar. (p51)

HELEN CATHCART/LONELY PLANET ©

**Jakov's Weinkeller** A favourite with stallholders from the nearby Naschmarkt. (p109)

**Melete Art Design Cocktails** Craft cocktails themed around changing art exhibitions. (p93)

**Kruger's American Bar** Sip a classic margarita in this 1920s, wood-panelled den. (p67)

**Barfly's Club** Terrific cocktails in an intimate setting. (p108)

**Blue Mustard** Stunning Vienna-inspired decor and cocktails. (p49)

## Best Microbreweries

**Siebensternbräu** Cheery brewpub with hoppy beers and a warm-weather courtyard. (p93)

**Salm Bräu** Relaxed spot right by Schloss Belvedere. (p129)

**1516 Brewing Company** Brews include a blueberry ale. (p68)

## Best Cocktails

**Loos American Bar** Mixology magic in this minimalist, Adolf Loos–designed bar. (p50)

## Worth a Trip

A hidden wonderland, convivial local *Heuriger* **Wieninger** (☎01-292 41 06; http://heuriger-wieninger.at; 21, Stammersdorfer Strasse 78; ⏰5pm-midnight Fri, from 2pm Sat, noon-10pm Sun Apr-mid-Dec; 🚌30A Freiheitsplatz) has a magical lantern- and candlelit garden draped with vines and a cosy, wood-panelled interior. Enjoy its light, fruity wines (mainly whites) alongside gourmet Austrian dishes.

# Treasure Hunt

*With a long-standing history of craftsmanship, Vienna has recently spread its creative wings in the fashion and design world. Whether you're browsing for hand-painted porcelain in the Innere Stadt, new-wave streetwear in Neubau or epicurean treats in the Freihausviertel, you'll find inspiration, a passion for quality and an eye for detail.*

## Shopping Streets

**Kärntner Strasse** The Innere Stadt's main shopping street and a real crowd-puller.

**Kohlmarkt** A river of high-end glitz, flowing into a magnificent Hofburg view.

**Neubau** Track down the city's hottest designers along boutique-clogged streets like Kirchengasse, Lindengasse and Neubaugasse.

**Mariahilfer Strasse** Vienna's mile of high-street style, with big names and crowds.

**Freihausviertel** Lanes packed with home-grown fashion, design and speciality food stores, south of Naschmarkt.

**Theobaldgasse** Hole-in-the-wall shops that purvey everything from fair-trade fashion to organic food.

## Markets

Almost every district has at least one market selling fresh produce from Monday to Saturday. Many markets reflect the ethnic diversity of their neighbourhood. Some host *Bauernmärkte* (farmers markets) on Saturday mornings, where growers from the surrounding countryside travel to the big city to sell their wares: fresh vegetables, tree-ripened fruit, cured hams, free-range eggs, homemade schnapps and cut flowers.

The city also hosts seasonal *Christkindlmärkte* (Christmas markets; p95) and springtime *Ostermärkte* (Easter markets). Along with festive decorations and handicrafts, there are food and drink stalls, and kids' activities.

### Best Markets

**Naschmarkt** Hands-down Vienna's best food market

MUELLEK JOSEF/SHUTTERSTOCK ©

and street food. (pictured; p111)

**Flohmarkt** Fabulous flea market. (p111)

**Brunnenmarkt** As buzzing as a Turkish bazaar. (p71)

## Best Food & Drink

**Staud's** Wine jellies, apricot jams and chutneys. (p71)

**Blühendes Konfekt** Say it with a bouquet of chocolate-dipped herbs or candied flowers. (p110)

**Wald & Wiese** Honey from Vienna's own rooftop apiaries. (p68)

**Zuckerlwerkstatt** Austrian sugar is used to make sweets based on traditional recipes. (p53)

## Best Fashion & Accessories

**Runway** Showcasing up-and-coming Austrian talent. (p95)

**Ina Kent** Silky soft leather bags made from vegetable-tanned leather. (p87)

**S/GHT** Austrian and international designers are stocked at this ahead-of-the-curve shop. (p87)

## Best Design

**Das Möbel** Furniture on the cusp of cool at a try-before-you-buy cafe. (p87)

**Die Werkbank** Design collective showcasing some of Vienna's most innovative creators. (p87)

## Top Shopping Tips

**Bargaining** Haggling is a no-no in shops, although you can certainly haggle when buying secondhand. It's a must at the *Flohmärkte* (flea markets).

**Taxes** *Mehrwertsteuer* (MWST; value-added tax) is 20% for most goods. Non-EU visitors can claim a MWST refund on purchases over €75.01. See www.globalblue.com for details.

# Coffee Houses

JULIAN LOVE/LONELY PLANET ©

*Vienna's long-standing tradition of coffee houses and cake shops captures the spirit of Gemütlichkeit – that quintessential Austrian quality of cosiness and languid indulgence. Grand or humble, poster-plastered or chandelier-lit, this is where you can join the locals for coffee, cake and a slice of living history.*

## Coffee-House Culture

In 2011 Vienna's *Kaffeehäuser* (coffee houses) were added to the Unesco list of Intangible Cultural Heritage, which defines them as 'places where time and space are consumed, but only the coffee is found on the bill'.

In 'Vienna's living rooms', the spirit of unhurried gentility remains sacrosanct. Meanwhile, a number of coffee houses are ushering in a new age of creativity.

## Coffee Decoder

Ask for 'a coffee' and you may get a puzzled look. The following are fixtures on most menus:

**Brauner** Black but served with a tiny splash of cream; comes in *gross* (large) or *klein* (small).

**Einspänner** Strong coffee with whipped cream, served in a glass.

**Verlängerter** A *Brauner* lengthened with hot water.

**Melange** The Viennese classic, half-coffee, half-milk and topped with milk froth or whipped cream, similar to a cappuccino.

**Kapuziner** With more milk than coffee and perhaps a sprinkling of grated chocolate.

**Mocca** Sometimes spelled *Mokka* or *Schwarzer* – black coffee.

**Eiskaffee** Cold coffee with vanilla ice cream and whipped cream.

**Maria Theresia** With orange liqueur and whipped cream.

**Türkische** Comes in a copper pot with coffee grounds and sugar.

## Best Historic Coffee Houses

**Café Sperl** A blast of nostalgia and a game of billiards in this *Jugendstil* (art nouveau) beauty. (p107)

ROSTISLAV AGEEV/SHUTTERSTOCK ©

**Café Leopold Hawelka** Hundertwasser and Warhol once hung out at this warm, wood-panelled cafe. (p49)

**Café Schwarzenberg** Magnificent coffee house on the Ringstrasse dating from 1861. (p108)

## Best Cakes

**Demel** Cakes and tortes fit for royalty. (pictured; p51)

**Café Sacher** King of the *Sacher Torte*. (p51)

**Diglas** Legendary *Apfel-strudel*. (p68)

**Vollpension** Intergenerational gem with a combined repertoire of 200 cake recipes. (p105)

## Best Free Live Music

**Café Prückel** Piano music plays from 7pm to 10pm on Monday, Wednesday and Friday in 1950s surrounds. (p61)

**Diglas** Bag a cosy booth to hear piano music from 7pm. (p68)

## Kaffeehäuser Essentials

**Prices** Expect to pay between €2 and €5 for a coffee, between €3 and €6 for a slice of cake, and around €9 for a main.

**Opening hours** Most open around 8am, and close between 7pm and midnight (earlier Sundays).

**Meals** Many *Kaffeehäuser* serve *Frühstuck* (breakfast) and a moderately priced lunchtime *Tagesteller* (dish of the day). Dishes are invariably hearty.

# Entertainment

*From opera, classical music and theatre to live rock or jazz, Vienna provides a wealth of entertainment opportunities. It is home to the German-speaking world's oldest theatre, the Burgtheater, as well as the famous Wiener Sängerknaben (Vienna Boys' Choir; pictured left) and the Vienna Philharmonic Orchestra, which performs in the acoustically superb Musikverein.*

## Opera

Vienna is a world capital for opera. The two main performance spaces are the Staatsoper, which closes in July and August, and Theater an der Wien, which remains open during these months.

## Classical Music

Opportunities to listen to classical music in Vienna abound. Churches are a hub for recitals of Bach and Händel especially, but also great venues for all sorts of classical music recitals.

## Rock & Jazz

Vienna's rock and jazz scene is lively, with local and international acts playing from the smallest bars to the largest arenas. See **Falter** (www.falter.at) for bands, venues and dates. The biggest bashes are the **Donauinselfest** (https://donauinselfest.at; admission free; ⏲late Jun) and **Jazz Fest Wien** (www.viennajazz.org; ⏲late Jun–mid-Jul).

## Standing-Room Tickets

Check with concert venues including the Staatsoper and Musikverein for details of purchasing inexpensive standing-room tickets.

## Cinema

*OF* or *OV* following a film title means it will screen in the original language; *OmU* original language with German subtitles; *OmenglU* and *OmeU* original language with English subtitles. Check listings at www.film.at.

## Best Classical

**Hofburg Concert Halls** The sumptuous Festsaal and Redoutensaal are regularly used for Strauss and Mozart concerts. (p52)

JONATHON STOKES/LONELY PLANET ©

**Staatsoper** One of the world's foremost opera houses. (p98)

**Musikverein** Home of the Vienna Philharmonic Orchestra. (p110)

**Konzerthaus** Major venue for classical music. (p130)

**Radiokulturhaus** Expect anything from odes to Sinatra and R.E.M. to evenings dedicated to Beethoven and Mozart. (p130)

**Burgkapelle** The Vienna Boys' Choir also sings Sunday Mass in this chapel. (p40)

## Best Theatre & Dance

**Volkstheater** One of Vienna's largest and grandest theatres. (p94)

**Vienna's English Theatre** Productions in English, from Shakespeare to contemporary works. (p94)

**Marionetten Theater** Enchanting puppet performances. (pictured right; p141)

**Tanzquartier Wien** Local and international dance performances. (p83)

## Best Rock & Jazz

**Konzerthaus** Hear a show in these hallowed halls. (p130)

**Jazzland** Long-standing venue with all jazz styles. (p68)

## Worth a Trip

Striking baroque meets contemporary concert hall **MuTh** (☎01-347 80 80; www.muth.at; 02, Obere Augartenstrasse 1e; Vienna Boys' Choir 5pm Fri performance €39-89; ⏰box office 4-6pm Mon-Fri & 1hr before performance; Ⓤ Taborstrasse) is the home of the Wiener Sängerknaben but, besides sessions with the angelic-voiced lads, the venue stages a top-drawer roster of dance, drama, opera, classical, rock and jazz performances.

# Architecture

KIEV.VICTOR/SHUTTERSTOCK ©

*Unwittingly, the Ottomans helped form much of Vienna's architectural make-up as seen today. The second Turkish siege saw the Habsburgs freed from the threat of war, and money previously spent on defence was poured into urban redevelopment, resulting in a frenzy of building in the baroque period in the 17th and early 18th centuries.*

## Rococo

Rococo, an elegant style incorporating pale colours and an exuberance of gold and silver, was all the rage in the 18th century.

## Neoclassical, Biedermeier & the Ringstrasse

From the 18th century (culminating in the 19th), Viennese architects – like those all over Europe – turned to a host of neoclassical architectural styles.

The end of the Napoleonic Wars and the ensuing celebration at the Congress of Vienna in 1815 ushered in the Biedermeier period (named after a satirical middle-class figure in a Munich paper). Viennese artists produced some extraordinary furniture during this period.

In the mid-19th century, Franz Josef I called for the fortifications to be demolished and replaced with a ring road lined with magnificent imperial buildings. Demolition of the old city walls began in 1857, and glorious buildings were created.

## Best Architectural Splendours

**Stephansdom** This soaring cathedral dominates Vienna's historic centre. (p56)

**Schloss Belvedere** Vienna's most sublime baroque palace. (p114)

**Hofburg** Six and a half centuries of imperial history. (p38)

**Schloss Schönbrunn** Baroque architectural beauty, garden grandeur. (p136)

**Rathaus** Vienna's neo-Gothic City Hall is the Ringstrasse's crowning glory. (p90)

Top: Secession (p104)

# Guided Tours

TRAVELVIEW/SHUTTERSTOCK ©

*Vienna offers some great opportunities for guided exploration. Join a tour by bus, tram, boat or on foot (perhaps on a specific theme), hop in a mini hot rod or aboard a Fiaker (horse-drawn carriage).*

**Fiaker Carriage Rides** (20min/40min/1hr tour €55/80/110; 10am-9pm) Traditional four-seater open carriages drawn by a pair of horses congregate at Heldenplatz at Hofburg, Stephansplatz and Albertinaplatz.

**Space & Place** (0680 125 43 54; www.spaceandplace.at; tours €10) Alternative English-language tours.

**Ring Tram** (01-712 46 83; www.wienerlinien.at; 01, Schwedenplatz, Platform C; adult/child €10/5; 10am-5.30pm; 1, 2 Schwedenplatz, U Schwedenplatz) Thirty-minute loop around the Ringstrasse (no stops).

**Hot Rod City Tour** (01-660 87 73; www.hotrod-tour-wien.com; 01, Judengasse 4; 2hr tour per person €99-119; 10am-8pm; 1, 2 Schwedenplatz, U Schwedenplatz) One-person mini hot rods cover a circuit of the city in convoy.

**Shades Tours** (Map p102, A3; 01-997 19 83; www.shades-tours.com; 07, Impact Hub Vienna, Lindengasse 56; walking tours €18; U Zieglergasse) Walks led by formerly homeless residents.

**Vienna Tour Guides** (www.wienguide.at; adult/child €17/8) Various themed guided walking tours.

**DDSG** (01-588 80; www.ddsg-blue-danube.at; 01, Schwedenbrücke; 1½-hour tours adult/child €23/11.50; hours vary; 1, 2 Schwedenplatz, U Schwedenplatz) Blue Danube Boats cover a variety of cruise routes.

## Looking after Fiaker Horses

Well-regulated measures to address animal-welfare concerns for the Fiaker-carriage horses were introduced in 2016 and include reducing service hours and stopping tours in 35°C-plus temperatures. Learn more on a Secrets of the Fiaker tour with **Riding Dinner** (0660 706 05 02; https://vienna.ridingdinner.com; tour per person €25, dinner tours per carriage from €295), which includes a tour of the stables.

# Activities

*Vienna steps between urban and outdoors without batting an eyelid. The Wienerwald to the west is crisscrossed with hiking and cycling trails, while the Danube, Alte Donau, Donauinsel and Lobau to the east offer boating, swimming, cycling and in-line skating. There are over 1200km of cycle paths, and the city is dotted with parks, some big (Prater), some small (Stadtpark).*

CREATIVEMARC/SHUTTERSTOCK ©

## Best Swimming

**Badeschiff** (www.badeschiff.at; 01, Danube Canal; adult/child €6.50/2; 9am-8pm May-Sep; 1, 2 Schwedenplatz, U Schwedenplatz) Floating on the bank of the Danube, this 28m-long summer lap pool has multiple decks with umbrella-shaded sun loungers.

**Strandbad Alte Donau** (22, Arbeiterstrandbadstrasse 91; adult/child €5.90/3.20; 9am-8pm Mon-Fri, from 8am Sat & Sun mid-May–mid-Sep; U Alte Donau) This bathing area makes great use of the Alte Donau during the summer months. Facilities include a restaurant and beach-volleyball court.

**Schönbrunnerbad** (01-817 53 53; www.schoenbrunnerbad.at; 13, Schloss Schönbrunn Schlosspark; adult/child half-day ticket €11/8, evening ticket €8/7; 8.30am-10pm Jun–mid-Aug, to 8pm mid-Aug–early Sep, to 7pm Apr, May & early Sep-early Oct; ; U Schönbrunn) The Schlosspark surrounding the Schönbrunn palace shelters this outdoor swimming complex, which has an Olympic-size (50m) pool for laps and a 25m recreation pool to splash about in, with a separated shallow area for kids. There are several saunas and a cafe.

## Best Ice Skating

**Wiener Eistraum** (www.wienereistraum.com; 01, Rathausplatz; adult/child from €8/5.50, preheated skate hire €7.50/5.50; 10am-10pm late Jan-early Mar; D, 1, 2, 71 Rathausplatz/Burgtheater, U Rathaus) In the heart of winter, Vienna's Rathausplatz transforms into two connected ice rinks covering a total of 9000 sq m (pictured). There are DJs, food stands, special events and *Glühwein* bars.

**Wiener Eislaufverein** (www.wev.or.at; 03, Lothringerstrasse 22; adult/child €7.30/6.30, boot hire €6.50; 9am-8pm Sat-Mon, to 9pm Tue-Fri; D Schwarzenbergplatz, U Stadtpark) This 6000 sq m open-air ice-skating rink is close to the Ringstrasse and Stadtpark.

# Under the Radar

*In Post-Covid Vienna, countless aspects of the visitor experience are bound to be different than they were before the pandemic struck. Here are a few tips on what you might want to do differently during your visit and what might be cool when the tourists finally return.*

ROMANBABAKIN/GETTY IMAGES ©

## Boutique Hotels in the Suburbs

Despite the pandemic, several new boutique hotels have opened in the suburbs of Vienna, places where there's somewhere to park and where prices may be a bit more 'local' than the extortionate city centre. The excellent public transport system means you'll have no problem reaching the city's main attractions.

## Hip Leopoldstadt

Ask locals in the know where the latest hip area of Vienna is located, and many will point you in the direction of the city's second district, Leopoldstadt. This diverse neighbourhood has some great global eateries as well as the Karmelitermarkt food market. Of course, it's also where you'll find Prater Park.

## Weird Museums

Vienna has some of the wackiest museums on the planet. The Museum of Art Fakes, the world's only Undertakers Museum, the Snowglobe Museum, the Museum of Contraception and Abortion and the Heat Museum are just some of the odd-ball attractions the Austrian capital offers.

## Meat-Free on the Danube

Vienna is repeatedly rated as one of the best cities in the world for those who prefer tofu schnitzel to the traditional veal variety. There are tens of vegetarian restaurants and an increasing number of vegan eateries – not bad for a country where meat consumption is high.

# For Kids

*Vienna is a wonderfully kid-friendly city. Children are welcomed in all aspects of everyday life, and many of the city's museums go out of their way to gear exhibitions towards them. Children's servings are typically available in restaurants, and, when kids need to burn off energy, playgrounds are plentiful.*

LEXAN/GETTY IMAGES ©

## Best Museums & Attractions for Kids

**Haus der Musik** Practical exhibits for almost all ages promote an understanding of music. (p64)

**Naturhistorisches Museum** Superb anthropology section where you can delve into forensics, plus overnight stays. (p84)

**Zoom** Exhibition sections and programs of hands-on arts and crafts (from eight months to 14 years old). (p83)

**Dschungel Wien** Children's theatre with dance and occasional English performances. (p83)

**Kindermuseum** Kids can dress up as princes and princesses at Schloss Schönbrunn's Children's Museum. (p140)

**Marionetten Theater** Performances of *The Magic Flute* and *Aladdin* take place at Schloss Schönbrunn's puppet theatre. (p141)

**Tiergarten** Kids will love visiting pandas, tigers and more at the world's oldest continuously operating zoo. (pictured; p141)

## Top Tips

**Public transport** Free for children under six years; half-price on single tickets under 15 years.

**Restaurants** Nappy changing facilities are rare. Dedicated kids' menus are also uncommon but children's servings are usually on offer.

**Hotels** Cots usually available. Children under 12 staying in their parents' room often receive discounts.

# Art

*Vienna is one of the world's most fascinating capitals when it comes to the visual arts. The Habsburg monarchs fostered and patronised the arts in grand style, leaving a rich legacy of fine historic paintings and sculptures. You'll encounter them all over the city, complemented today by modern and contemporary works.*

VVOEVALE/GETTY IMAGES ©

## Jugendstil & the Secession

Vienna's branch of the Europe-wide Art Nouveau movement was known as *Jugendstil* ('Youthful Style').

By the second decade of the 20th century, many artists were moving towards a uniquely Viennese style, called Secession, which stripped away some of the more decorative aspects of *Jugendstil*.

No one embraced the sensualism of *Jugendstil* and Secessionism more than Gustav Klimt one of Vienna's most famous artists.

## Contemporary Arts

Vienna has a thriving contemporary-arts scene with a strong emphasis on confrontation, pushing boundaries and exploring new media.

Standing in stark contrast to the more self-consciously daring movements such as Actionism, Vienna's extensive Neue Wilde group emphasises traditional techniques and media.

## Best Museums & Galleries

**Kunsthistorisches Museum Vienna** Packed with Old Masters. (p74)

**Albertina** Exceptional collection of graphic art. (p44)

**Schloss Belvedere** Home to the world's largest Klimt collection. (p114)

**Leopold Museum** Vast collection of mainly 19th-century and modernist Austrian artworks. (p81)

**MUMOK** Vienna's finest collection of 20th-century art; Viennese Actionism is regularly displayed. (p81)

**Secession** At this showcase of the Secessionists, the biggest draw is Klimt's gilded *Beethoven Frieze*. (p104)

# Four Perfect Days

## Day 1

GREG ELMS/LONELY PLANET ©

Start at Vienna's heart, the **Stephansdom** (pictured; p56) and be awed by the cathedral's cavernous interior, Gothic stone pulpit and baroque high altar. Climb the cathedral south tower for skyline views or delve below ground into its ossuary, the Katakomben (catacombs).

Head to the **Hofburg** (p38) and soak up the grandeur of this Habsburg architectural masterpiece. Narrow it down to one or two of the museums here, such as the **Kaiserappartements** (p39), containing the Sisi Museum.

Finish in the cobblestoned Spittelberg district at enduring favourites such as old-school brewery **Siebensternbräu** (p93) and hip bars like vintage-furnished **Liebling** (p91).

## Day 2

TUPUNGATO/SHUTTERSTOCK ©

Make your way to the **Kunsthistorisches Museum Vienna** (pictured; p74), where you can plan on spending at least a whole morning in the thrall of its Old Masters.

The afternoon is a good time to change artistic direction and explore at least one of the museums in the **MuseumsQuartier** (p80). The light, bright Leopold Museum has splendid Austrian art. MUMOK makes a complete contrast, with contemporary, often controversial works.

Explore the Innere Stadt's illuminated streets and lively bar scene in the evening in the centre, hitting architectural treasures such as **Zwölf Apostelkeller** (p68) or **Kruger's American Bar** (p67).

MRGB/SHUTTERSTOCK ©

## Day 3

Divide your morning between the magnificently landscaped French-style formal gardens and art-filled galleries of **Schloss Belvedere** (p114).

Make your way to the **Prater** (pictured; p132), Vienna's playground of woods, meadows and sideshow attractions at the Würstelprater. The highlight here is the 19th-century Riesenrad Ferris wheel, famed for its role in 1949 film *The Third Man,* as well as the James Bond instalment *The Living Daylights* and art-house favourite *Before Sunrise*.

Leopoldstadt is fast becoming one of Vienna's hippest districts, with an increasing number of cafes and bars popping up. Finish the evening at 18th-storey restaurant/cocktail bar **Das Loft** (p11) with a sweeping panorama of the city.

JORG HACKEMANN/SHUTTERSTOCK ©

## Day 4

Take an eye-popping tour of baroque extravaganza **Schloss Schönbrunn** (p136), and stroll the French formal gardens.

Browse the **Naschmarkt** (pictured; p111) for picnic supplies or stop at one of its sit-down restaurants, before visiting another baroque jewel, the **Karlskirche** (p104). Then head to **Secession** (p104) to see seminal works by members of the Vienna Secession including Klimt's 34m-long *Beethoven Frieze*.

The Margareten (the 5th district) and Mariahilf (the 6th), both flanking the trickling Wien River, offer plenty of drinking and nightlife opportunities. Sip *Sekt* (sparkling wine) at **Sekt Comptoir** (p101) and hit the dance floor at **Club U** (p109).

# Need to Know

For detailed information, see Survival Guide (p143)

**Currency**
Euro (€)

**Language**
German

**Visas**
Generally not required for stays of up to 90 days; from 2023, non-EU nationals need ETIAS pre-authorisation.

**Money**
ATMs are plentiful. Credit cards aren't always accepted in budget hotels, budget to midrange restaurants, or bars and cafes.

**Mobile Phones**
Check with your service provider about using your phone in Austria and roaming costs.

**Time**
Central European Time (GMT/UTC plus one hour)

**Tipping**
Rounding up for drinks, around 10% for meals and taxis.

## Daily Budget

### Budget: Less than €100

Dorm bed: €25–30

Cheap double per person: €40–65

Self-catering or lunchtime specials: €7.50–12

Free sights and cheap museums: to €8

Happy hour: beer/wine €2–4, cocktails €4.50–7.50

### Midrange: €100–180

Hotel double per person: €65–110

Two-course midrange meal with glass of wine: €25–35

High-profile museums: €13

### Top end: More than €180

Upmarket hotel double per person: from €110

Multicourse meal with wine: from €70

Opera or theatre: from €40

## Advance Planning

**Three months before** Reserve tickets for Staatsoper seating, Vienna Boys' Choir, the Spanish Riding School and major events.

**One month before** Make reservations for top-shelf restaurants; check upcoming events at www.wien.info and venue websites. Book accommodation in summer and during the Christmas market season.

**One week before** Check Falter (www.falter.at) for drinking and dining tips, and reserve a table in popular restaurants for weekend nights.

## Arriving in Vienna

### Vienna International Airport

The City Airport Train (CAT; Map p102; www.cityairporttrain.com; single/return €11/19; 1 Landstrasse-Wien Mitte, U Landstrasse) leaves the airport every 30 minutes from 6.09am to 11.39pm, 365 days. The cheaper but slower S7 suburban train (€4.20, 37 minutes) also runs every 30 minutes from 5.18am to 12.18am from the airport to Wien-Mitte. It's €25 to €50 for a taxi.

### Wien Hauptbahnhof

Situated 3km south of Stephansdom, Vienna's gleaming main train station handles all international trains, those from Austria's provincial capitals, and many local and regional trains. It's linked to the centre by U-Bahn line 1, trams D and O, and bus 13A. A taxi to the centre costs about €10.

## Getting Around

### U-Bahn

Fast, comfortable and safe. Trains run from 5am to midnight Monday to Thursday and continuously from 5am Friday through to midnight Sunday.

### Tram

Slower but more enjoyable. Depending on the route, trams run from around 5.15am to about 11.45pm.

### Bus

Reliable, punctual, with several very useful routes for visitors. Most run from 5am to midnight, though services can be sporadic or nonexistent on weekends.

### Night Bus

Especially useful for outer areas; runs every 30 minutes from 12.30am to 5am.

TRABANTOS/SHUTTERSTOCK ©

# Vienna Neighbourhoods

**Hofburg & Around (p37)**
The rambling Hofburg palace complex, home to a cache of museums and the famous Spanish Riding School, is the centrepiece of this stately neighbourhood.

**The Museum District & Neubau (p73)**
Art fills this neighbourhood's masterpiece-packed museums, its design ateliers and cutting-edge restaurants and bars.

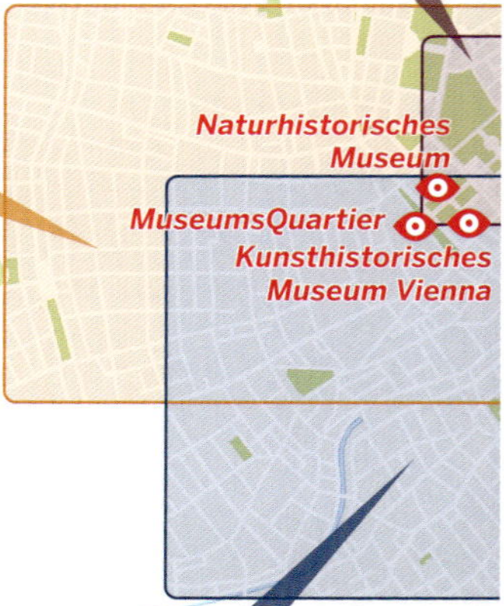

**Karlsplatz (p97)**
The vibrant Karlsplatz neighbourhood harbours tantalising markets, artisan shops, lively nightlife venues and outstanding entertainment venues.

**Historic Centre (p55)**
Elegant shopping streets, musical pilgrimages, and absorbing Roman and Jewish sites are all key draws of Vienna's ancient heart.

**Schloss Belvedere to the Canal (p113)**
The monumental Schloss Belvedere is the trophy sight of this leafy neighbourhood, which also has standout architecture and creative enterprises.

# Explore Vienna



## Vienna's Walking Tours



View from Stephansdom (p56) VERONICKA/SHUTTERSTOCK ©

Explore

# Hofburg & Around

*Vienna's imperial splendour peaks in this part of the Innere Stadt (city centre), where Fiaker (horse-drawn carriages) rumble along curved, cobbled streets. Its centrepiece is the magnificent Hofburg palace complex, which brims with museums and world-famous attractions including the waltzing horses of the Spanish Riding School. Museums also abound in the streets north towards Stephansplatz.*

## The Short List

- ***Hofburg (p38)*** *Strolling through the monumental Hofburg palace complex.*
- ***Albertina (p44)*** *Viewing world-class graphic art within luxurious palace rooms.*
- ***Kaiserappartements (p39)*** *Touring the Habsburg imperial apartments, the Sisi Museum, dedicated to Empress Elisabeth, and the Silberkammer (Silver Depot).*
- ***Spanish Riding School (p40)*** *Catching the famous white Lipizzaner stallions during a mesmerising equine ballet performance.*
- ***Neue Burg Museums (p41)*** *Revelling in the historical musical instruments, arms and armour, and ancient artefacts unearthed during Austrian archaeologists' excavations at Ephesus in Turkey.*

## Getting There & Around

U Herrengasse (U3) and Stephansplatz (U1, U3) are closest to the Hofburg, but Museumsquartier (U2) can also be convenient for the Heldenplatz side of the palace complex.

Useful for entering from Ringstrasse (D, 1, 2, 71 Ring/Volkstheater, Burgring and Kärntner Ring/Oper).

**Hofburg & Around Map on p42**

**Hofburg and gardens (p38)** ROMAN BABAKIN/SHUTTERSTOCK ©

Top Experience

# Lord it Up at Royal Hofburg

*Built as a fortified castle in the 13th century, the Hofburg has been the home of the Habsburg rulers from Rudolph I in 1279 until the Austrian monarchy collapsed under Karl I in 1918, and is the ultimate display of Austria's former imperial power. Today the impressive palace complex contains the offices of the Austrian president, an ensemble of extraordinary museums and stately public squares.*

MAP P42, D3

Imperial Palace

01-533 75 70

www.hofburg-wien.at

01, Michaelerkuppel

D, 1, 2, 71 Burgring, U Herrengasse

NSAFONOV/SHUTTERSTOCK ©

## Kaiserappartements

The **Kaiserappartements** (Imperial Apartments; ☎01-533 7570; 01, Michaelerplatz; adult/child €15/9, incl admission to the Sisi Museum and the Silberkammer; incl guided tour €18/10.50; ⏰9am-6pm Jul & Aug, to 5.30pm Sep-Jun) were once the official living quarters of Franz Joseph I (1830–1916) and Empress Elisabeth, or Sisi, as she was affectionately named (1837–98). The highlight is the **Sisi Museum** (☎01-533 75 70; adult/child €15/9, incl guided tour €18/10.50; ⏰9am-6pm Jul & Aug, to 5.30pm Sep-Jun), devoted to Austria's most beloved empress, which has a strong focus on the clothing and jewellery of Austria's monarch and a replica of her personal fitness room complete with rings and bars. Also here is a reconstruction of Sisi's luxurious Pullman coach. Many of the empress' famous portraits are also on show, as is her death mask, made after her assassination in Geneva in 1898.

Multilingual audio guides are included in the admission price. Guided tours take in the Kaiserappartements, the Sisi Museum and the adjoining **Silberkammer** (Silver Depot, Imperial Silver Collection; ☎01-533 75 70; adult/child €15/9, incl guided tour €18/10.50; ⏰9am-6pm Jul & Aug, to 5.30pm Sep-Jun) – its largest silver service caters to 140 dinner guests.

## Kaiserliche Schatzkammer

The **Kaiserliche Schatzkammer** (Imperial Treasury; ☎01-525 24-0; www.kaiserliche-schatzkammer.at; 01, Schweizerhof; adult/child €12/free; ⏰9am-5.30pm Wed-Mon) contains secular and ecclesiastical treasures of priceless value and splendour – the sheer wealth of this collection of crown jewels is staggering. As you walk through the rooms you see a golden rose, diamond-studded Turkish sabres, a 2680-carat Colombian emerald and, the highlight of the treasury, the imperial crown. The wood-panelled **Sacred Treasury** has a collection of

### ★ Top Tips

- If you plan to visit several attractions in and around the Hofburg palace, it's worth getting a combination ticket (p46). These tickets not only invariably save you money but will also save you time spent queuing for individual tickets.
- Book several months ahead for Spanish Riding School performances and at least a month ahead for standing-room tickets.

### ✕ Take a Break

Stop for a classic Viennese sausage at Bitzinger Würstelstand am Albertinaplatz (p47).

Take a seat on the terrace or in the art-nouveau interior of the beautiful **Palmenhaus** (☎01-533 10 33; www.palmenhaus.at; 01, Burggarten; ⏰10am-midnight Mon-Fri, from 9am Sat, 9am-11pm Sun; 🚋D, 1, 2, 71 Burgring, Ⓤ Karlsplatz, Museumsquartier) for a drink or a traditional Austrian meal.

rare religious relics: fragments of the True Cross, the Holy Lance that pierced Jesus on the Cross, one of the nails from the Crucifixion, a thorn from Christ's crown and a piece of tablecloth from the Last Supper. Multilingual audio guides cost €5 (the shorter highlight audio tour is free) and are very worthwhile.

## Burgkapelle

The **Burgkapelle** (Royal Chapel; ☎01-533 99 27; www.hofmusikkapelle.gv.at; 01, Schweizerhof; ⏰10am-2pm Mon & Tue, 11am-1pm Fri) dates from the 13th century. It received a Gothic makeover from 1447 to 1449, but much of this disappeared during the baroque fad. Its vaulted wooden statuary survived and is testament to those Gothic days. The **Vienna Boys' Choir Mass** (☎01-533 992 711; www.hofmusikkapelle.gv.at; 01, Schweizerhof; tickets €11-37) takes place here every Sunday at 9.15am between September and June. The chapel is sometimes closed to visitors in July and August, so check ahead in those months.

## Spanish Riding School

The world-famous **Spanish Riding School** (Spanische Hofreitschule; ☎01-533 90 31-0; www.srs.at; 01, Michaelerplatz 1; tickets €27-225, standing room €13; ⏰hours vary) is a Viennese institution truly reminiscent of the imperial Habsburg era. This unequalled equestrian show is performed by Lipizzaner stallions formerly kept at an imperial stud established at Lipizza (hence the name). These graceful stallions perform an equine ballet to classical music as chandeliers shimmer above.

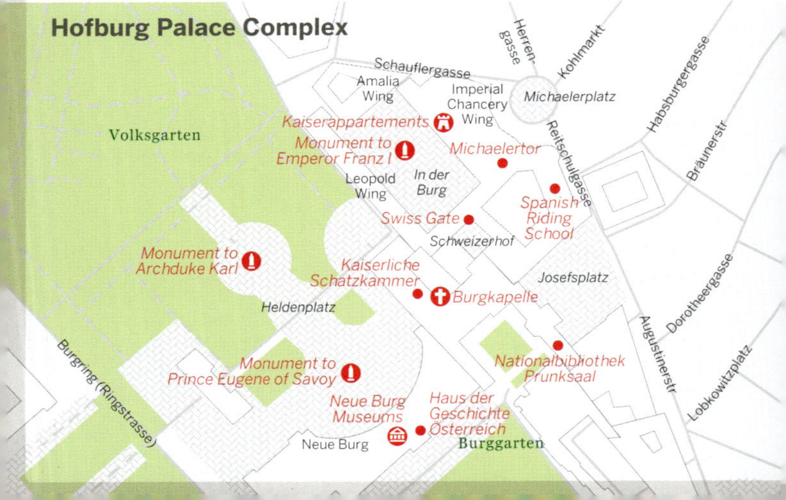

There are many different ways to see the Lipizzaner. Performances are the top-shelf variant, and for seats at these you will need to book several months in advance. The website lists performance dates and you can order tickets online. As a rule of thumb, performances are at 11am on Sunday from mid-February to June and mid-August to December, with frequent additional performances on Saturday and occasionally other days of the week. For standing-room tickets, book at least one month in advance. During the summer break, it hosts special 'Piber meets Vienna' performances. Visitors to the **Morgenarbeit** can drop in for part of a session (morning training sessions; adult/child €15/7.50, 10am to noon mid-August to June).

One-hour **guided tours** (adult/child €18/9; 2pm, 3pm and 4pm Tuesday to Sunday), held in English and German, take you into the performance hall, stables and other facilities. A combined **morning training and tour** (adult/child €31/15) is another option. The visitor centre here sells all tickets.

## Neue Burg Museums

One ticket covers entry to three **Neue Burg Museums** (☎01-525 24-0; www.khm.at; 01, Heldenplatz; adult/child €16/free; ⏰10am-6pm Fri-Wed, to 9pm Thu Jun-Aug, closed Wed Sep-May; 🚋D, 1, 2, 71 Burgring, U Herrengasse, Museumsquartier). The **Sammlung alter Musikinstrumente** (Collection of Ancient Musical Instruments) contains a wonderfully diverse array of instruments. The **Ephesos Museum** features artefacts unearthed during Austrian archaeologists' excavations at Ephesus in Turkey between 1895 and 1906. The **Hofjagd- und Rüstkammer** (Arms and Armour) museum contains ancient armour dating mainly from the 15th and 16th centuries. An audio guide costs €5.

## Haus der Geschichte Österreich

Austria's first museum of contemporary history opened in 2018. The **Haus der Geschichte Österreich** (hdgö; House of Austrian History; ☎01-534 10-805; www.hdgoe.at; 01, Heldenplatz; adult/child €8/free; ⏰10am-6pm Tue, Wed & Fri-Sun, to 9pm Thu; 🚋D, 1, 2, 71 Burgring) spans the period from the mid-19th century to the present. Exhibits, documents, photos and films cover political, cultural, economic and social history, including the First Republic's 1918 founding, Nazi occupation, migrations, protest culture, democracy and science. The evolving collection includes, for example, a football used in a 2018 friendly match against Germany, which Austria won. English-language guided tours lasting 1½ hours depart at 3pm on Saturdays (adult/child €4/free).

A
B
C
D
1
2
3
4
5
6
Rathausplatz
Rathausplatz Burgtheater
Bankgasse
Herrengasse
Strauchgasse
Rathauspark
Universitätsring (Ringstrasse)
Minoritenplatz
Leopold-Figl-Gasse
Löwelstr
Herrengasse
5
Globenmuseum
B-Kreisky-Gasse
Stadiongasse/ Parlament
Schauflergasse
Ballhaus-platz
Volksgarten
Dr-Karl-Renner-Ring (Ringstrasse)
Hofburg
In der Burg
Dr Karl-Renner-Ring
Ring Volkstheater
17
Heldenplatz
Bellariastr
23
Naturhistorisches
Maria-Theresien-Platz
Heldenplatz
Burgring (Ringstrasse)
For reviews see
Top Experiences p38
Sights p44
Eating p47
Drinking p49
Entertainment p52
Shopping p52
8
Burggarten
Burgring
Babenbergerstr
Jugendinfo
0 200 m
0 0.1 miles
N

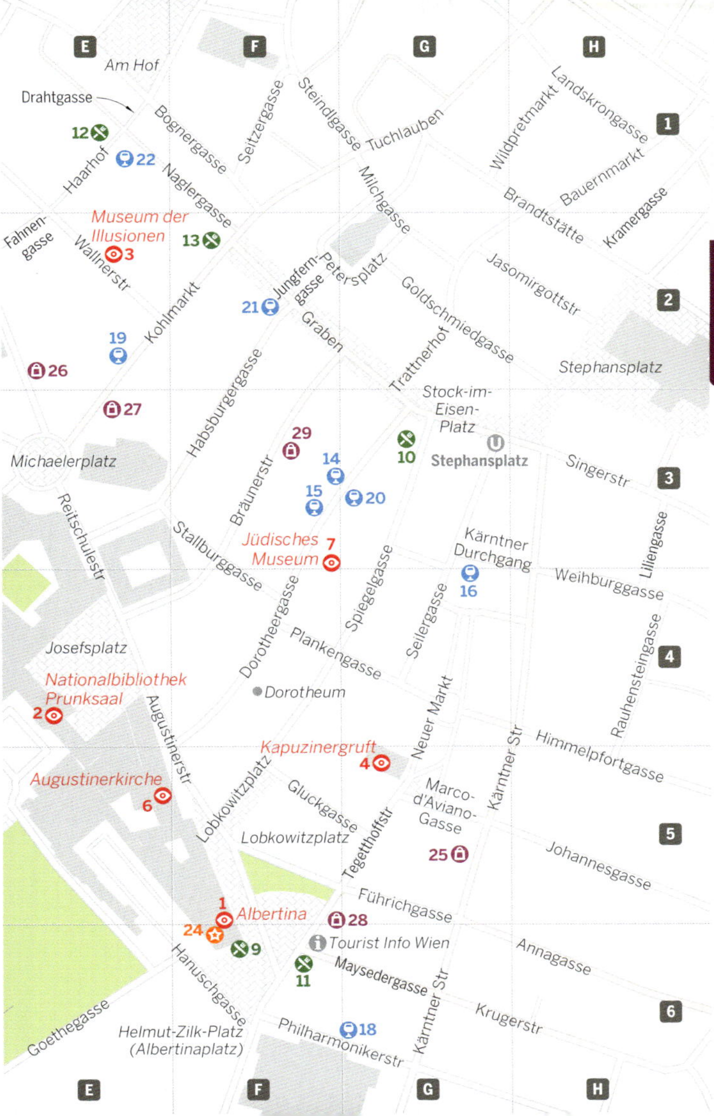
E
F
G
H
1
2
3
4
5
6
Am Hof
Drahtgasse
Bognergasse
Seitzergasse
Steindlgasse
Tuchlauben
Wildpretmarkt
Landskrongasse
Bauernmarkt
12
22
Haarhof
Naglergasse
Milchgasse
Brandtstätte
Kramergasse
Fahnengasse
Museum der Illusionen
3
13
Wallnerstr
Jungferngasse
Petersplatz
Goldschmiedgasse
Jasomirgottstr
21
Graben
Kohlmarkt
19
26
Trattnerhof
Stephansplatz
27
Stock-im-Eisen-Platz
Habsburgergasse
29
10
Stephansplatz
Michaelerplatz
Bräunerstr
14
Singerstr
15
20
Reitschulestr
Stallburggasse
Jüdisches Museum
7
Kärntner Durchgang
Liliengasse
16
Weihburggasse
Spiegelgasse
Dorotheergasse
Seilergasse
Plankengasse
Josefsplatz
Nationalbibliothek Prunksaal
2
Dorotheum
Neuer Markt
Rauhensteingasse
Augustinerstr
Kapuzinergruft
4
Kärntner Str
Himmelpfortgasse
Augustinerkirche
6
Lobkowitzplatz
Gluckgasse
Marco-d'Aviano-Gasse
Lobkowitzplatz
Tegetthoffstr
25
Johannesgasse
Führichgasse
1
Albertina
28
24
9
Tourist Info Wien
Annagasse
11
Maysedergasse
Hanuschgasse
Goethegasse
Krugerstr
Kärntner Str
18
Helmut-Zilk-Platz (Albertinaplatz)
Philharmonikerstr

# Sights

## Albertina

GALLERY

1 MAP P42, F5

Once used as the Habsburgs' imperial apartments for guests, the Albertina is now a repository for an exceptional collection of graphic art. The permanent Batliner Collection – with over 100 paintings covering the period from Monet to Picasso – and the high quality of changing exhibitions make the Albertina highly worthwhile.

Multilingual audio guides (€4) cover all exhibition sections and tell the story behind the apartments and the works on display. (01-534 830; www.albertina.at; 01, Albertinaplatz 1; adult/child €16/free; 10am-6pm Sat-Tue & Thu, to 9pm Wed & Fri; D, 1, 2, 71 Kärntner Ring/Oper, U Karlsplatz, Stephansplatz)

## Nationalbibliothek Prunksaal

LIBRARY

2 MAP P42, E4

Austria's flagship library, the Nationalbibliothek, contains an astounding collection of literature, maps, globes of the world and other cultural relics; its highlight, though, is the **Prunksaal** (Grand Hall), a majestic baroque hall built between 1723 and 1726, with a fresco by Daniel Gran. Commissioned by Karl VI (whose statue is under the central dome), the library holds some 200,000 leather-bound scholarly tomes. Audio guides cost €3. (01-534 10; www.onb.ac.at; 01, Josefsplatz 1; adult/child €8/free; 10am-6pm Fri-Wed, to 9pm Thu Jun-Sep, closed Mon Oct-May; D, 1, 2, 71 Burgring, U Herrengasse)

## Museum der Illusionen

MUSEUM

3 MAP P42, E2

Vienna's mind-bending Museum of Illusions, opened in 2017, confounds your senses through its 40 interactive optical illusions and installations. They include stereograms (3D pictures with 'hidden' objects), tilted rooms, mirages, a giant kaleidoscope, an infinity room, and a tunnel with spinning images on the walls that make it impossible to keep your balance (despite the central walkway not moving). It's fascinating for kids and adults alike. (Museum of Illusions; 01-532 22 55; www.museumderillusionen.at; Wallnerstrasse 4; adult/child €12/8; 10am-8pm; U Herrengasse)

## Kapuzinergruft

MAUSOLEUM

4 MAP P42, G5

Beneath the **Kapuzinerkirche** (Church of the Capuchin Friars; www.erzdioezese-wien.at; 01, Tegethoffstrasse 2; 8am-6pm), the Kapuzinergruft is the final resting place of most of the Habsburg royal family, including Empress Elisabeth. Opened in 1633, it was instigated by Empress Anna (1585–1618). Her body and that of her husband, Emperor Matthias (1557–1619), were the first entombed in this impressive vault. A total of 149 Habsburgs are buried here, including 12 emperors and 19 empresses.

Only three Habsburgs are notable for their absence here. The last emperor, Karl I, was buried in exile in Madeira, and Marie Antoinette still lies in Paris. The third is Duc de Reichstadt, son of Napoleon's second wife, Marie Louise, who was transferred to Paris as a publicity stunt by the Nazis in 1940.

Also on display are rows of urns containing the internal organs of the Habsburgs. One of the many privileges of being a Habsburg was to be dismembered and dispersed after death: their hearts are in the Augustinerkirche in the Hofburg and the rest of their bodies are in the Kapuzinergruft. English-language, hour-long guided tours take place at 3.30pm Wednesday to Saturday. (Kaisergruft; www.kapuzinergruft.com; 01, Tegethoffstrasse 2; adult/child €7.50/4.50, incl guided tour €10.50/7.50; 10am-6pm Fri-Wed, from 9am Thu; U Stephansplatz)

## Globenmuseum

MUSEUM

5 MAP P42, D2

Part of the Nationalbibliothek collection of museums, along with the **Esperantomuseum** (01, Herrengasse 9, ground fl) and Papyrus museum. Admission covers all three and audio guides cost €3. This small museum situated inside a former palace (Palais Mollard) is dedicated to cartography. Among the collection of 19th-century globes and maps are some gems dating from the

Kapuzinergruft

KARL ALLEN LUGMAYER/SHUTTERSTOCK ©

## Combination Museum Tickets

There are lots of combined options for visiting the Hofburg and nearby museums.

**Sisi Ticket** (adult/child €34/21) Includes the Imperial Apartments, Sisi Museum and Silberkammer (Imperial Silver Collection) with an audio guide, as well as Schloss Schönbrunn and the Hofmobiliendepot (Imperial Furniture Collection).

**Neue Burg Museums** (adult/child €16/free) Includes the Neue Burg Museums' Sammlung Alter Musik Instrumente (Collection of Ancient Musical Instruments), Ephesos Museum and Hofjagd- und Rüstkammer (Arms and Armour) museum, and the Kunsthistorisches Museum Vienna.

**Annual ticket Kunsthistorisches Museum Vienna** (adult/child €44/25) Includes the Kunstkammer, Kunsthistorisches Museum Vienna, Neue Burg Museums, Kaiserliche Schatzkammer, Wagenburg, Schloss Ambras Innsbruck and Theatermuseum.

**Schatz der Habsburger** (Treasures of the Habsburgs; adult/child €22/free) Includes the Kunsthistorisches Museum Vienna, Neue Burg Museums and Kaiserliche Schatzkammer.

**Masterticket** (adult/child €24/free) Includes the Neue Burg Museums, Kunsthistorisches Museum Vienna and the Leopold Museum.

**Die Kostbarkeiten des Kaisers** (Treasures of the Emperors; adult/child €24/free) Includes the Kaiserliche Schatzkammer and Morgenarbeit (morning training sessions) at the Spanish Riding School.

**Nationalbibliothek Universal-Wochenticket** (€16.50) Includes entry to the Nationalbibliothek's Esperantomuseum, Globenmuseum and Papyrusmuseum, the Nationalbibliothek Prunksaal and the Literaturmuseum. Valid for seven days.

16th century. Look for the globe made for Emperor Karl V by Mercator in 1541. (01-534 10-425; www.onb.ac.at; 01, Herrengasse 9, 1st fl; adult/child €5/free; 10am-6pm Tue, Wed & Fri-Sun, to 9pm Thu; D, 1, 2, 71 Burgring, U Herrengasse)

### Augustinerkirche

CHURCH

6 MAP P42, E5

The real highlight of the 14th-century Gothic Augustinerkirche is not its pale, vaulted interior but the Herzgruft, a crypt containing silver urns with the hearts of

54 Habsburg rulers. The crypt is open on Sundays after the 11am Mass (celebrated with a full choir and orchestra) – turn up around 12.30pm.

The church hosts regular evening classical music concerts; check schedules at http://hochamt.augustiner.at. Sometimes on a visit you can catch the choir practising. Many Habsburg weddings took place here. (Augustinian Church; ☎01-533 70 99; http://augustinerkirche.augustiner.at; 01, Augustinerstrasse 3; ⊙7.30am-5.30pm Mon, Wed & Fri, to 7.15pm Tue & Thu, 9am-7.30pm Sat & Sun; U Stephansplatz, Herrengasse)

### Jüdisches Museum MUSEUM

7 ⊙ MAP P42, F3

Housed inside Palais Eskeles, Vienna's Jüdisches Museum showcases the history of Jews in Vienna, from the first settlements at Judenplatz in the 13th century to the present. Spaces devoted to changing exhibitions are complemented by the permanent exhibition covering 1945 to the present day; the highlight is the startling collection of ceremonial art on the top floor. Multimedia guides cost €4. Combined tickets to the Jüdisches Museum and Museum Judenplatz (p65) are valid for four days. (Jewish Museum; ☎01-535 04 31; www.jmw.at; 01, Dorotheergasse 11; adult/child incl Museum Judenplatz €12/free; ⊙10am-6pm Sun-Fri; U Stephansplatz)

### Burggarten GARDENS

8 ⊙ MAP P42, D6

Tucked behind the Hofburg, the Burggarten is a leafy oasis amid the hustle and bustle of the Ringstrasse and Innere Stadt. The marble statue of Mozart is the park's most famous tenant, but there's also a statue of Franz Joseph in military garb.

Lining the Innere Stadt side of the Burggarten is the **Schmetterlinghaus** (Butterfly House; ☎01-533 85 70; www.schmetterlinghaus.at; 01, Burggarten; adult/child €7/4; ⊙10am-4.45pm Mon-Fri, to 6.15pm Sat & Sun Apr-Oct, to 3.45pm Nov-Mar; U Karlsplatz) and the beautiful *Jugendstil* Palmenhaus (p39) bar. (Castle Garden; www.bundesgaerten.at; 01, Burgring; admission free; ⊙6am-10pm Apr-Oct, 7.30am-5.30pm Nov-Mar; 🚋D, 1, 2, 71 Burgring, U Museumsquartier)

## Eating

### Bitzinger Würstelstand am Albertinaplatz STREET FOOD €

9 MAP P42, F6

Behind the Staatsoper, Vienna's best sausage stand has cult status. Bitzinger offers the contrasting spectacle of ladies and gents dressed to the nines, sipping beer, wine or Joseph Perrier champagne while tucking into sausages at outdoor tables or the heated counter after performances. Mustard comes in *Süss* (sweet, ie mild) or *Scharf* (fiercely hot). (www.bitzinger-wien.at; 01, Albertinaplatz; sausages

€3.50-4.70; 8am-4am; D, 1, 2, 71 Kärntner Ring/Oper, U Karlsplatz, Stephansplatz)

## Trześniewski

SANDWICHES €

10 MAP P42, G3

Trześniewski has been serving exquisite open-faced finger-style sandwiches since 1902. Choose from 22 delectable toppings incorporating primarily Austrian-sourced produce – chicken liver; smoked salmon and horseradish cream cheese; wild paprika and red pepper; egg and cucumber – on dark Viennese bread. This branch is the flagship of a now 11-strong chain in Vienna. (www.trzesniewski.at; 01, Dorotheergasse 1; 1/8 sandwiches €1.40/8.40; 8.30am-7.30pm Mon-Fri, 9am-6pm Sat, 10am-5pm Sun; U Stephansplatz)

## Café Mozart

CAFE €€

11 MAP P42, F6

Opening to a covered terrace, 1794-established Café Mozart serves classic Viennese cakes including *Apfelstrudel* (apple strudel), *Esterhazy Torte* (layered almond cake), *Sacher Torte* (chocolate cake with apricot jam) and *Rehrücken* (chocolate-almond mousse dipped in dark chocolate). More substantial dishes span *Tafelspitz* (boiled beef) with creamed spinach potato salad to beef goulash with bread dumplings. (01-241 00-200; www.cafe-mozart.at; 01, Albertinaplatz 2; mains €14-32, cakes & pastries €4.50-8.50, mains €14-32; kitchen 8am-11.30pm, bar to midnight; ; U Karlsplatz)

## Bierhof

AUSTRIAN €€

12 MAP P42, E1

A narrow passageway opens to a courtyard where umbrella-shaded tables beneath the trees make a charming spot to dine on homemade classics like *Eiernockerl* (flour-and-egg dumplings), *Tiroler Gröstl* (pork, potatoes and bacon, topped with a fried egg), *Tiroler Leber* (liver dumplings with apple sauce and green beans) and *Wiener Schnitzel* (Viennese cutlet) with parsley potatoes. The midweek lunch menu costs just €7.90. (01-533 44 28; www.bierhof.at; 01, Haarhof 3; mains €11-25; 11.30am-10pm Mon-Sat, to 9pm Sun; ; U Herrengasse)

## Meinl's Restaurant

INTERNATIONAL €€€

13 MAP P42, F2

Meinl's combines cuisine of superlative quality with an unrivalled wine list and views of Graben. Creations at its high-end restaurant span calamari and white-truffle risotto, and apple-schnapps-marinated pork fillet with green beans and chanterelles. The providore, **Julius Meinl am Graben** (8am-7.30pm Mon-Fri, 9am-6pm Sat), has a cafe and a sushi bar, and the cellar wine bar serves great-value lunch menus. (01-532 33 34 6000; www.meinlamgraben.at; 01, Graben 19; mains €27-39, 4-course menus €79; 8am-11pm Mon-Fri, from 9am Sat; ; U Stephansplatz)

# Drinking

## Café Leopold Hawelka

COFFEE

14 MAP P42, F3

Opened in 1939 by Leopold and Josefine Hawelka, whose son Günter and grandsons Amir and Michael still bake the house-speciality *Buchteln* (jam-filled, sugar-dusted yeast rolls) to the family's secret recipe, this low-lit, picture-plastered coffee house is a living slice of Viennese history. Artists and writers who have hung out here included Friedensreich Hundertwasser, Elias Canetti, Arthur Miller and Andy Warhol. (www.hawelka.at; 01, Dorotheergasse 6; 8am-midnight Mon-Thu, to 1am Fri & Sat, 10am-midnight Sun; U Stephansplatz)

## Blue Mustard

COCKTAIL BAR

15 MAP P42, F3

Backlit wooden hand carvings of Stephansdom's Gothic windows and a wall-to-wall neon-lit map of Vienna make this one of the city's coolest bars. Sensational craft cocktails vary seasonally, and might include the Donau (absinthe, apricot schnapps, blueberry-infused gin and pineapple juice), the Sisi (Jägermeister, chocolate liqueur and cream) and the Habsburg (Goldschläger – cinnamon liqueur with gold leaf – triple sec, soda and lime). (01-934 67 05; www.bluemustard.at; 01, Dorotheergasse 6-8; 5pm-2am Tue-Thu, to 4am Fri & Sat; ; U Stephansplatz)

Hofburg Concert Hall (p52)

GLOWIMAGES/GETTY IMAGES ©

## Composers at a Glance

Just some of the composers who lived and worked in this musical city include the following:

**Christoph Willibald Gluck** (1714–87) Major works include *Orfeo* (1762) and *Alceste* (1767).

**Wolfgang Amadeus Mozart** (1756–91) Wrote some 626 pieces; among the greatest are *The Marriage of Figaro* (1786), *Così fan Tutte* (1790) and *The Magic Flute* (1791).

**Joseph Haydn** (1732–1809) Wrote 108 symphonies, 68 string quartets, 47 piano sonatas and about 20 operas.

**Ludwig van Beethoven** (1770–1827) Studied briefly with Mozart in Vienna in 1787; he returned in late 1792. Major works include the Symphony No 9 in D Minor, Symphony No 5 and late string quartets.

**Franz Schubert** (1797–1828) Schubert was born and bred in Vienna. His best-known works are his last symphony (the Great C Major Symphony), his Mass in E-flat and the *Unfinished Symphony.*

**The Strausses & the Waltz** The early masters of the genre were Johann Strauss the Elder (1804–49) and Josef Lanner (1801–43). Johann Strauss the Younger (1825–99) composed over 400 waltzes, including 'The Blue Danube' (1867).

**Johannes Brahms** (1833–97) At the age of 29, Brahms moved to Vienna, where many of his works were performed by the Vienna Philharmonic Orchestra.

**Gustav Mahler** (1860–1911) Known mainly for his nine symphonies; particularly Symphony Nos 1, 5 and 9.

### Loos American Bar COCKTAIL BAR

16 MAP P42, G4

Loos is *the* spot in the Innere Stadt for a classic cocktail such as its signature dry martini, expertly whipped up by talented mixologists. Designed by Austrian architect Adolf Loos in 1908, this tiny 27-sq-metre box (seating just 20 or so patrons) is bedecked from head to toe in onyx, marble, mahogany and polished brass, with space-enhancing mirrored walls. (www.loosbar.at; 01, Kärntner Durchgang 10; noon-4am; U Stephansplatz)

### Volksgarten ClubDiskothek CLUB

17 MAP P42, B4

Spilling onto the Volksgarten's lawns, these early-19th-century premises are split into three areas:

the Wintergarten lounge bar with vintage 1950s furnishings and palms; Cortic Säulenhalle (column hall), hosting live music and theme nights; and the hugely popular ClubDiskothek. Check the agenda online. (www.volksgarten.at; 01, Burgring 1; 9pm-6am Thu, from 11pm Fri & Sat Apr–mid-Sep; D, 1, 2, 71 Ring/Volkstheater, U Museumsquartier, Volkstheater)

### Café Sacher

COFFEE

18 MAP P42, G6

With a battalion of waiters and an air of nobility, this grand cafe is celebrated for its *Sacher Torte*, a wonderfully rich iced-chocolate cake with apricot jam once favoured by Emperor Franz Joseph. For the full-blown experience, head to the opulent chandelier-lit interior. There's also a covered pavement terrace, and a 1920s-styled tearoom, Sacher Eck, serving the same menu next door. (www.sacher.com; 01, Philharmonikerstrasse 4; 8am-midnight; D, 1, 2, 71 Kärntner Ring/Oper, U Karlsplatz)

### Demel

CAFE

19 MAP P42, E2

Within sight of the Hofburg, this elegant and regal cafe has a gorgeous rococo-period salon. Demel's specialities include the *Annatorte* (a calorie bomb of cream and nougat) and the *Fächertorte* (with apples, walnuts, poppy seeds and plum jam). The window displays an ever-changing array of edible art pieces (ballerinas and manicured bonsai, for example). (www.demel.at; 01, Kohlmarkt 14; 8am-7pm; 1A, 2A Michaelerplatz, U Herrengasse, Stephansplatz)

### Kaffee Rösterei Hawelka

COFFEE

20 MAP P42, G3

Hawelka's headquarters in Vienna's southwest roasts beans that supply its famous Café Leopold Hawelka (p49) as well as this 2019-opened, contemporary cafe-shop with a full-length glass facade. Sip a coffee in-house or buy beans to take away. (www.hawelka.at; 01, Dorotheergasse 7; 10am-6pm Tue-Sun; U Stephansplatz)

### Villon

WINE BAR

21 MAP P42, F2

This 500-year-old wine cellar is sunk 16m deep into the ground, so forget all about your mobile phone working. Spanning four levels, the interior is smart and modern, with light-coloured woods in the main room where you can order wine by the glass or bottle, accompanied by Parmesan cheese, bread, olives and the Viennese speciality Thun ham. (www.villon.at; 01, Habsburgergasse 4; 11am-11pm Mon-Sat; U Herrengasse, Stephansplatz)

### Esterházykeller

WINE BAR

22 MAP P42, E1

Tucked in a quiet courtyard just off Kohlmarkt, this *Heurigen* (wine tavern) has an enormous rustic cellar – complete with medieval weaponry and farming tools – where excellent wine (and beer) is served direct from the Esterházy Palace wine estate in Eisenstadt. The adjoining Esterházy Stüberl (restaurant; mains €10.90 to €26.90) opens from 11am to 11pm. (☎01-533 34 82; www.esterhazykeller.at; 01, Haarhof 1; ⊙5-11pm; U Stephansplatz, Herrengasse)

# Entertainment

## Hofburg Concert Halls

CLASSICAL MUSIC

23 MAP P42, D4

The Neue Hofburg's concert halls, the sumptuous Festsaal and Redoutensaal, are regularly used for Strauss and Mozart concerts, featuring the Hofburg Orchestra and soloists from the Staatsoper and Volksoper. Seating is not allocated, so get in early to secure a good seat. (☎01-587 25 52; www.hofburgorchester.at; 01, Heldenplatz; ⊙8.30pm performances; tickets €45-110, available online; 🚋D, 1, 2, 71 Burgring, U Herrengasse)

### Auction House

The **Dorotheum** (Map p42, F4; www.dorotheum.com; 01, Dorotheergasse 17; ⊙10am-6pm Mon-Fri, 9am-5pm Sat; U Stephansplatz) is among the largest auction houses in Europe. For the casual visitor it's more like a museum, housing everything from antique toys and tableware to autographs, antique guns and, above all, lots of quality paintings. You can bid at the regular auctions held here; otherwise just drop by and enjoy browsing.

## Österreichisches Filmmuseum

CINEMA

24 MAP P42, F6

Situated inside the Albertina (p44), the Austrian Film Museum shows a range of films with and without subtitles in the original language, featuring a director, a group of directors or a certain theme from around the world in programmes generally lasting a couple of weeks. Screenings are usually at 6.45pm; check the website for other times. (Austrian Film Museum; ☎01-533 70 54; www.filmmuseum.at; 01, Auginerstrasse 1; adult/child €10.50/6; ⊙film screenings Sep-early Jun; 🚋D, 1, 2, 71 Kärntner Ring/Oper, U Karlsplatz)

# Shopping

## J&L Lobmeyr Vienna

HOMEWARES

25 MAP P42, G5

Reached by a beautifully ornate wrought-iron staircase, this is one of Vienna's most lavish retail experiences. The collection of Biedermeier pieces, Loos-designed sets, fine/arty glassware and porcelain on display here glitters from the lights of the chandelier-festooned atrium. Lobmeyr has been in business since 1823, when it exclusively supplied the imperial court. (www.lobmeyr.at; 01, Kärntner Strasse 26; ⌚10am-7pm Mon-Fri, to 6pm Sat; U Stephansplatz)

### Zuckerlwerkstatt FOOD & DRINKS

26 MAP P42, E2

Long-lost recipes for traditional sweets and all-natural ingredients including Austrian sugar (produced from sugar beet) are used by this 'sugar workshop'. Its pillow-shaped striped silk candies, sugar drops, fruit jellies, lollipops, candy canes and boiled sweets are enticingly displayed in glass jars. (www.zuckerlwerkstatt.at; 01, Herrengasse 6-8; ⌚10am-6pm Mon-Fri, 9am-5pm Sat; U Herrengasse)

### Rozet und Fischmeister JEWELLERY

27 MAP P42, E3

Founded in 1770, Rozet und Fischmeister supplied the imperial court, and is today run by the sixth generation of the same family. It uses time-honoured techniques to create exquisite jewellery, as well as silverware. Restoration, repairs and engraving can be arranged. (www.rozetundfischmeister.at; 01, Kohlmarkt 11; ⌚10am-1pm & 2-6pm Mon-Fri, 10am-3pm Sat; U Herrengasse)

### Bonbons Anzinger CHOCOLATE

28 MAP P42, F5

This jewel box of a chocolate shop has a dazzling array of handmade truffles and pralines, Bonbons Anzinger has a tiny upstairs tearoom serving coffee, tea and hot chocolate, with a chocolate on the side. Its speciality is the *Mozartkugel*, a dark-chocolate-covered ball filled with pistachio marzipan and nougat, along with gingerbread at Christmas. (www.bonbons-anzinger.at; 01, Tegetthoffstrasse 7; ⌚10am-6pm Mon-Sat, noon-4pm Sun; 🚋D, 1, 2, 71 Kärntner Ring/Oper, U Karlsplatz)

### Gmundner CERAMICS

29 MAP P42, F3

Gmundner has been manufacturing ceramics by hand since 1492, and it's estimated over half of Austrian households hold at least one Gmundner piece. Its plates, casserole dishes, tea and coffee cups and more are all safe to use in microwaves and dishwashers. If you're nervous about transporting these beautiful wares in your luggage, international shipping can be arranged. (www.gmundner.at; 01, Bräunerstrasse 3; ⌚10am-6.30pm Mon-Fri, to 5pm Sat; U Stephansplatz)

Explore

# Historic Centre

*Vienna's heart beats in the streets surrounding its most distinctive landmark, the towering Gothic cathedral Stephansdom. The oldest part of the city, with a tangle of cobbled lanes and elegant thoroughfares graced with pastel-shaded baroque buildings, this epicentral neighbourhood takes in the medieval Jewish quarter in the northwest, the stretch down to Danube Canal's southern bank and the areas northeast and east of Stephansplatz.*

## The Short List

- ***Stephansdom (p56)*** *Marvelling at the intricate details of Vienna's famous Gothic cathedral.*
- ***Literaturmuseum (p64)*** *Getting acquainted with Austria's literary luminaries and their seminal works.*
- ***Museum Judenplatz (p65)*** *Viewing the excavated remains of the medieval synagogue that stood on this site and learning about Vienna's Jewish history.*
- ***Mozarthaus Vienna (p64)*** *Visiting Wolfgang Amadeus Mozart's only surviving Viennese home, where he composed* The Marriage of Figaro.
- ***Haus der Musik (p64)*** *Conducting your own virtual orchestra and engaging with other interactive exhibits at this innovative music museum.*

## Getting There & Around

U Stephansplatz (U1, U3) and Schwedenplatz (U1, U4) – and to a lesser extent Stubentor (U3), Herrengasse (U3) and Karlsplatz (U1, U2, U4) – are the main stops.

Schwedenplatz (1, 2) and Kärntner Ring/Oper (1, 2, D, 71) are the most convenient stops.

**Historic Centre Map on p62**

**Stephansdom (p56)** BLUEJAYPHOTO/GETTY IMAGES ©

Top Experience

# Marvel at Stephansdom

*Soaring above the surrounding cityscape, Vienna's immense, filagreed Gothic masterpiece Stephansdom – or Steffl (Little Stephen) as it's locally (and ironically) dubbed – symbolises the city like no other building. Highlights include the cathedral's spectacular main nave with its Gothic stone pulpit and baroque high altar, its Katakomben (catacombs), two towers and the cathedral treasures.*

MAP P62, B4

St Stephen's Cathedral

www.stephanskirche.at

01, Stephansplatz

9-11.30am & 1-4.30pm Mon-Sat, 1-4.30pm Sun, English tours 10.30am Mon-Sat

U Stephansplatz

## History

A church has stood on this site since the 12th century, reminders of which today are the Romanesque **Riesentor** (Giant Gate) and **Heidentürme** (Towers of the Heathens) at the entrance and above it. In 1359 at the behest of Habsburg Duke Rudolf IV, Stephansdom began receiving its Gothic makeover and Rudolf earned himself the epithet 'The Founder' by laying the first stone in the reconstruction.

## Stephansdom: Inside & Out

From outside the cathedral, the first thing that will strike you is the glorious tiled roof, with its dazzling row of chevrons on one end and the Austrian eagle on the other.

Inside the cathedral, the magnificent Gothic stone pulpit takes pride of place, fashioned in 1515 by Anton Pilgrim (his likeness appears in the stonework). The pulpit railing is adorned with salamanders and toads, symbolising the battle of good against evil.

At the far end of the main nave, the baroque high altar shows the stoning of St Stephen. The chancel to its left has the winged Wiener Neustadt altarpiece, dating from 1447; the right chancel has the Renaissance red-marble tomb of Friedrich III. Under his guidance the city became a bishopric (and the church a cathedral) in 1469.

## Stephansdom Katakomben

The area around the cathedral was originally a graveyard. But with plague and influenza epidemics striking Europe in the 1730s, Karl VI ordered the graveyard be closed and henceforth Vienna buried its dead beneath Stephansdom in the Katakomben. Today, they contain the remains of countless victims, which are kept in a mass grave and a bone house. Look out too for urns containing the

### ★ Top Tips

- Admission to the side aisle (on the left, facing the altar) is free if you only want to gain a quick impression of the cathedral.
- For worshippers only, the main nave is free to enter during Mass. Outside these times, the main nave is open to the public by audio-guided and guided tours (p59).
- Along with the main nave, the *Katakomben* and lift to the north tower are closed during Mass (held up to eight times daily).
- An all-inclusive tour (p59) gives a greater overview of this Gothic wonder.

### ✕ Take a Break

Tuck into huge schnitzels at **Figlmüller** (☎01-512 61 77; www.figlmueller.at; 01, Wollzeile 5; mains €13-20.50; ⏰11am-9.30pm; 📶; U Stephansplatz), a beloved Vienna *Beisl* (small tavern).

Habsburgs' remains, though their hearts are in the Hofburg's Augustinerkirche (p46). Entrance is allowed only on a tour.

## Cathedral South Tower

When the foundation stone for the **Südturm** (South Tower; adult/child €5/2; 9am-5.30pm) was laid in 1359, Rudolf IV is said to have used a trowel and spade made of silver. Two towers were originally envisaged here, but the Südturm grew so high that little space remained for the second; in 1433 the tower reached its final height of 136.7m. Today you can ascend the 343 steps to a small platform for one of Vienna's most spectacular views over the rooftops of the Innere Stadt; you don't need a tour ticket for the main nave.

## Cathedral Pummerin

Weighing 21 tonnes, the **Pummerin** (Boomer Bell; adult/child €6/2.50; 9am-5.30pm) is Austria's largest bell and was installed in the 68.3m-high north tower in 1957. While the rest of the cathedral was rising up in its new Gothic format, work was interrupted on this tower due to a lack of cash and the fading allure of Gothic architecture. It's accessible only by lift; you don't need a tour ticket for the main nave.

## Dom- & Diözesanmuseum

The **Dom- & Diözesanmuseum** (Cathedral & Diocesan Museum of Vienna; www.dommuseum.at; 01, Stephansplatz 6; adult/child €8/3; 10am-6pm Wed & Fri-Sun, to 8pm Thu) is a treasure trove of religious art pieces spanning a period of

Stephansdom interior

more than 1000 years. Among the collection's extraordinary exhibits are the earliest European portrait – of Duke Rudolf IV (1360) – and two Syrian glass vessels (1280–1310), thought to be among the oldest glass bottles in the world.

## Guided Tours & Music

### Multilingual Audio-Guide Tour

The most common option to see the cathedral interior. Audio guides (adult/child cost €6/2.50) are available from 9am to 11.30am and 1pm to 4.30pm Monday to Saturday, and from 1pm to 4.30pm Sunday.

### Guided Tours in English & German

English-language tours explain the background of the cathedral and walk you through its main interior features. The 30-minute tours leave at 10.30am Monday to Saturday (adult/child €6/2.50). The same guided tours in German leave at 3pm daily.

### All-Inclusive Tour

All-inclusive tours are partly with an audio guide, partly with a tour guide (adult/child €14.90/3.90). Tours take in the cathedral interior, Katakomben, south tower and north tower. Children aren't allowed to do it alone. Total time is 2½ hours; they're available from 9am to 5.30pm daily.

### Evening Roof-Walk Tours in English & German

These 75-minute tours (adult/child €11/5) depart at 7pm every Saturday from July to September (weather permitting) and feature a brisk climb to the top of the south tower and a walk along the exterior rain gutter with close-up views of the roof and panoramas of the city.

### Special Events & Mass

The website www.dommusik-wien.at has a programme of special concerts and events, but the 10.15am Mass on Sundays (9.30am during the school holidays around July and August) is something special, as it's conducted with full choral accompaniment. Tickets are available online at www.kunstkultur.com.

VITALYEDUSH/GETTY IMAGES ©

Walking Tour

# An Evening Out on the Town

*Vienna's Innere Stadt has a wealth to see by day, but an evening stroll through its sepia-toned streets, passing floodlit monuments like the Stephansdom, provides a much-more-local perspective. You'll drink local wines, dine on Viennese specialities and see films from the Austrian Film Archive; you can also join the Viennese for late-night ice cream.*

## Walk Facts

**Start** Vinothek W-Einkehr (1, 2, 31 Schwedenplatz, U Schwedenplatz)

**End** Zanoni & Zanoni (U Stephansplatz)

**Length** 1.6km; two to four hours

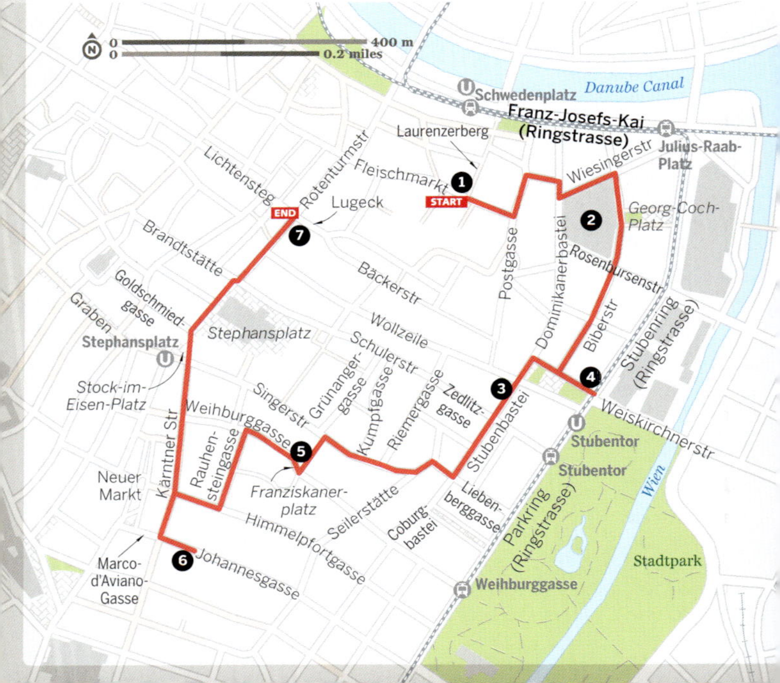

## ❶ Pre-Dinner Drink

Join the crowds milling outside tiny wine bar **Vinothek W-Einkehr** (☎0676 408 28 54; www.w-einkehr.at; 01, Laurenzerberg 1; ⏲4-10pm Tue-Sat), whose wines are from renowned Austrian wine-growing regions.

## ❷ Jugendstil Design

Beautifully illuminated at night, the marble-cased and metal-'studded' **Postsparkasse** (www.ottowagner.com; 01, Georg-Coch-Platz 2; admission free; ⏲10am-5pm Mon-Fri) building is the *Jugendstil* work of Otto Wagner, who oversaw its construction between 1904 and 1906, and again from 1910 to 1912.

## ❸ Dinner

*Tafelspitz* (boiled beef) is among Vienna's most renowned dishes, and white-tableclothed restaurant **Plachutta** (☎01-512 15 77; www.plachutta-wollzeile.at; 01, Wollzeile 38; mains €19-27.20; ⏲11.30am-11.15pm) serves 13 varieties from different cuts of Austrian-reared beef, such as *Mageres Meisel* (lean, juicy shoulder meat), *Beinfleisch* (larded rib meat) and *Lueger Topf* (shoulder meat with beef tongue and calf's head).

## ❹ Dessert

**Café Prückel** (www.prueckel.at; 01, Stubenring 24; ⏲8.30am-10pm; 📶) features an intact 1950s design. Intimate booths, strong coffee and Prückel's speciality, its crispy, flaky *Apfelstrudel* (apple strudel) served with cream, are all big drawcards. From 7pm to 10pm on Mondays, Wednesdays and Fridays you'll catch live piano music.

## ❺ Digestif

Bohemian **Kleines Café** (01, Franziskanerplatz 3; ⏲10am-2am; 🚋2 Weihburggasse) recalls Vienna's inspired *Jugendstil* days. Space is limited inside, but there's wonderful summer outdoor seating on a cobbled square overlooking the baroque Franziskanerkirche.

## ❻ Movie Time

The **Metro Kinokulturhaus** (☎01-512 18 03; www.filmarchiv.at; 01, Johannesgasse 4; film tickets €8.50, exhibition tickets €7.50, combined ticket €13; ⏲3-9pm) hosts exhibitions from the Austrian Film Archive's vast collection. First converted for screenings in 1924, the restored cinema here retains its wood panelling and red-velvet interior, and is an atmospheric place to catch historic and art-house Austrian films (in German).

## ❼ Ice Cream

Late-opening Italian gelateria and pasticceria **Zanoni & Zanoni** (www.zanoni.co.at; 01, Lugeck 7; ice cream per 1/2/3/4 scoops €1.30/2.30/3.20/3.90; ⏲7.30am-midnight) scoops up 30 seasonal varieties of gelato.

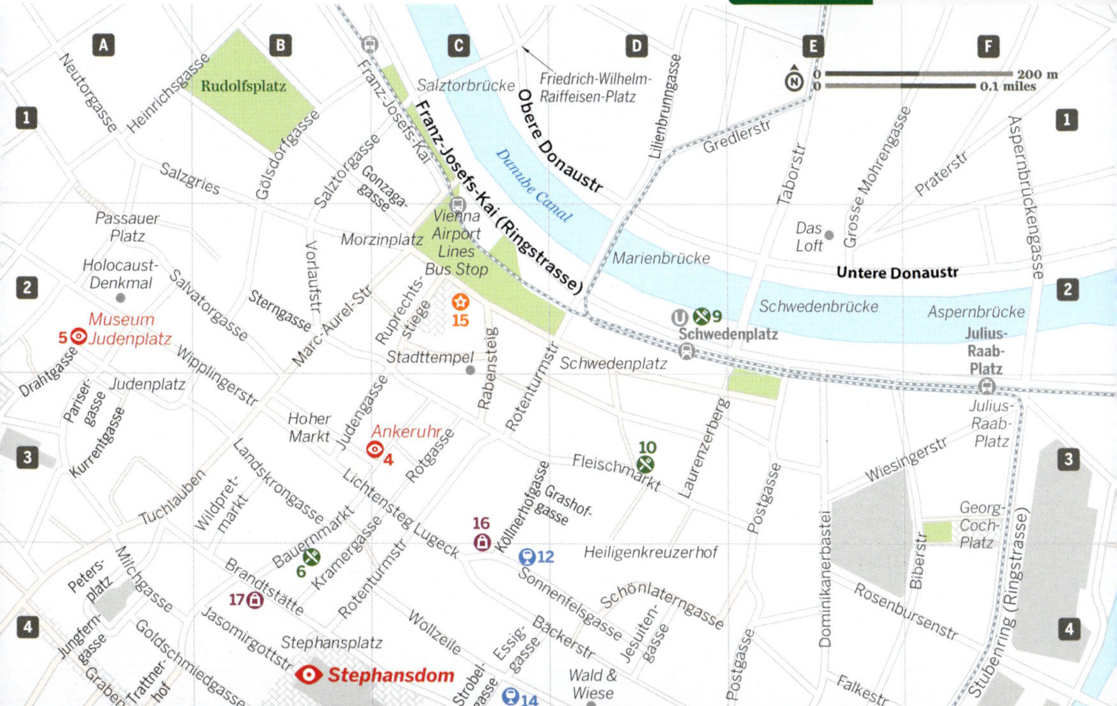
A
B
C
D
E
F
1
2
3
4
0 200 m
0 0.1 miles
Rudolfsplatz
Neutorgasse
Heinrichsgasse
Gölsdorfgasse
Salzgries
Salztorgasse
Gonzaga-gasse
Franz-Josefs-Kai
Franz-Josefs-Kai (Ringstrasse)
Salztorbrücke
Obere Donaustr
Friedrich-Wilhelm-Raiffeisen-Platz
Danube Canal
Lilienbrunngasse
Gredlerstr
Taborstr
Grosse Mohrengasse
Praterstr
Aspernbrückengasse
Das Loft
Untere Donaustr
Marienbrücke
Schwedenbrücke
Aspernbrücke
Julius-Raab-Platz
Schwedenplatz
9
Passauer Platz
Holocaust-Denkmal
Morzinplatz
Vienna Airport Lines Bus Stop
Vorlaufstr
Salvatorgasse
Sterngasse
Marc-Aurel-Str
Ruprechts-stiege
15
Stadttempel
Rabensteig
Rotenturmstr
5 Museum Judenplatz
Drahtgasse
Judenplatz
Wipplingerstr
Pariser-gasse
Kurrentgasse
Hoher Markt
Judengasse
Ankeruhr 4
Rotgasse
Fleischmarkt
10
Laurenzerberg
Postgasse
Wiesingerstr
Julius-Raab-Platz
Georg-Coch-Platz
Biberstr
Dominikanerbastei
Rosenbursenstr
Stubenring (Ringstrasse)
Tuchlauben
Wildpret-markt
Landskrongasse
Lichtensteg
Lugeck
Bauernmarkt
6
Kramergasse
Rotenturmstr
16
Köllnerhofgasse
Grashof-gasse
12
Heiligenkreuzerhof
Sonnenfelsgasse
Schönlaterngasse
Jesuiten-gasse
Peters-platz
Milchgasse
17
Brandstätte
Jungfern-gasse
Graben
Trattner-hof
Goldschmiedgasse
Jasomirgottstr
Stephansplatz
Stephansdom
Wollzeile
Essig-gasse
Bäckerstr
Strobel-gasse
14
Wald & Wiese
Postgasse
Falkestr

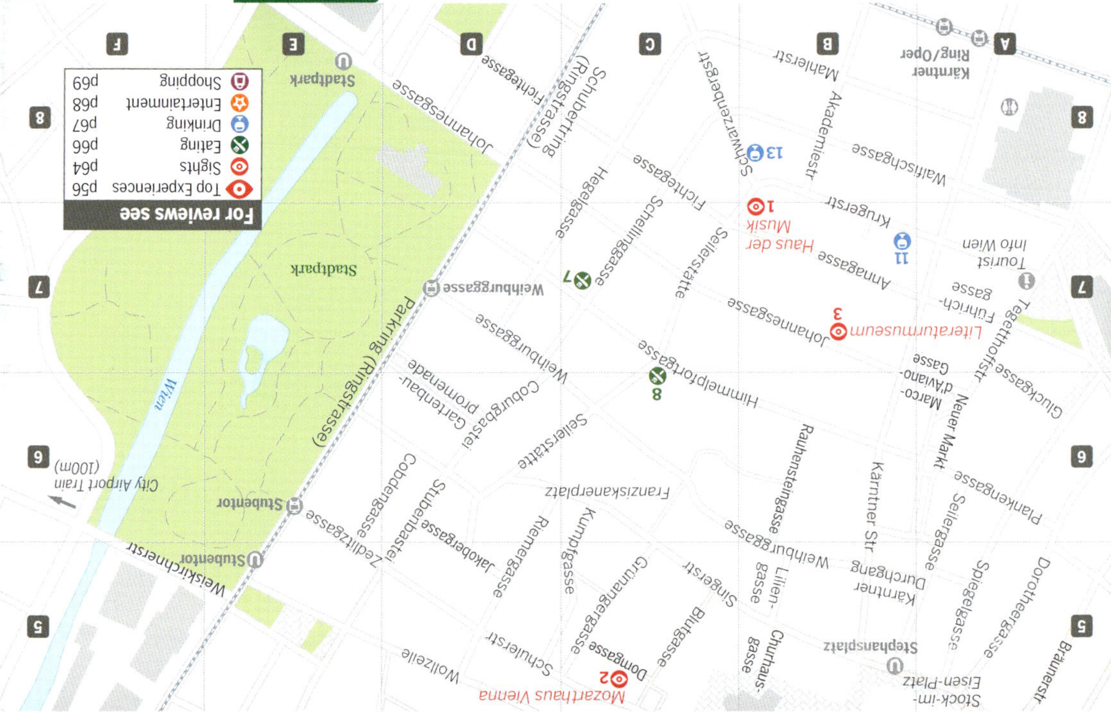
For reviews see
Top Experiences p56
Sights p64
Eating p66
Drinking p67
Entertainment p68
Shopping p69
A
B
C
D
E
F
5
6
7
8
City Airport Train (100m)
Wien
Stadtpark
Stadtpark
Stubentor
Stubentor
Weiskirchnerstr
Parkring (Ringstrasse)
Schubertring (Ringstrasse)
Weihburggasse
Johannesgasse
Fichtegasse
Hegelgasse
Schellinggasse
Seilerstätte
Haus der Musik
1
13
Schwarzenbergstr
Mahlerstr
Akademiestr
Walfischgasse
Krugerstr
Annagasse
11
Tourist Info Wien
Kärntner Ring/Oper
Literaturmuseum
3
Führich-gasse
Tegetthoffstr
Gluckgasse
Marco-d'Aviano-Gasse
Neuer Markt
Himmelpfortgasse
8
7
Weihburggasse
Coburgbastei
Gartenbau-promenade
Seilerstätte
Franziskanerplatz
Rauhensteingasse
Kärntner Str
Plankengasse
Seilergasse
Weihburggasse
Lilien-gasse
Kärntner Durchgang
Spiegelgasse
Dorotheergasse
Bräunerstr
Stephansplatz
Stock-im-Eisen-Platz
Churhaus-gasse
Singerstr
Blutgasse
Grünangergasse
Domgasse
Mozarthaus Vienna
2
Kumpfgasse
Riemergasse
Jakobergasse
Stubenbastei
Cobdengasse
Zedlitzgasse
Schulerstr
Wollzeile

# Sights

## Haus der Musik

MUSEUM

1 MAP P62, B7

The Haus der Musik explains the world of sound and music to adults and children alike (in English and German) in an amusing and interactive way. Exhibits are spread over four floors and cover everything about how sound is created, from Vienna's Philharmonic Orchestra to street noises. The staircase between floors acts as a piano; its glassed-in ground-floor courtyard hosts musical events. After 8pm, adult admission drops to €6.50. (www.hausdermusik.com; 01, Seilerstätte 30; adult/child €13/6, incl Mozarthaus Vienna €18/8; 10am-10pm; ; 2, 71 Schwarzenbergplatz, U Karlsplatz)

## Mozarthaus Vienna

MUSEUM

2 MAP P62, C5

The great composer spent close to three happy and productive years at this residence between 1784 and 1787. Exhibits include copies of music scores and paintings, while free audio guides recreate the story of his time here. Mozart spent a total of 11 years in Vienna, changing residences frequently and sometimes setting up his home outside the Ringstrasse in the cheaper *Vorstädte* (inner suburbs) when his finances were tight. Of these, the Mozarthaus Vienna is the only one that survives. ( 01-512 17 91; www.mozarthaus vienna.at; 01, Domgasse 5; adult/child €11/4.50, incl Haus der Musik €18/8; 10am-7pm; U Stephansplatz)

## Literaturmuseum

MUSEUM

3 MAP P62, B7

An 1844 Biedermeier building houses Austria's literature museum, which opened in 2015. It contains books, manuscripts, letters, photos, illustrations and personal effects (such as desks) from the country's most seminal authors, playwrights and poets, from the 18th century to the present day. The celebrated writers represented include Günther Anders, Ingeborg Bachmann, Peter Handke, Robert Menasse, Herta Müller and Hilde Spiel. You can also hear readings and quotations from the museum's 550 hours of audio recordings. Information leaflets are available in English. (Literature Museum; www.onb.ac.at/museen/literaturmuseum; 01, Grillparzerhaus, Johannesgasse 6; adult/child €7/free; 10am-6pm Tue, Wed & Fri-Sun, to 9pm Thu; U Stephansplatz)

## Ankeruhr

MONUMENT

4 MAP P62, C3

A *Jugendstil* masterpiece created by Franz von Matsch in 1911, this mechanical clock was named after the Anker Insurance Co, which commissioned it. Over a 12-hour period figures including Roman Emperor Marcus Aurelius (who died in Vienna in 180 CE), Joseph Haydn, Prince Eugene of Savoy and Maria Theresia pass across the clock face, indicating the time against a static measure showing the minutes. At noon, all the figures trundle past in succession to organ. (Anker Clock; 01, Hoher Markt 10-11; U Stephansplatz, Schwedenplatz)

### Museum Judenplatz

MUSEUM

5 MAP P62, A2

The main focus of Museum Judenplatz is on the excavated remains of a medieval synagogue that once stood on Judenplatz, with a film and numerous exhibits to elucidate Vienna's Jewish history. It was built in the Middle Ages, but Duke Albrecht V's 'hatred and misconception' led him to order its destruction in 1421. The basic outline of the synagogue can still be seen here. Combined tickets to the Museum Judenplatz and Jüdisches Museum (p47) are valid for four days. (01-535 04 31; www.jmw.at; 01, Judenplatz 8; adult/child incl Jüdisches Museum €12/free; 10am-6pm Sun-Thu, to 5pm Fri; ; U Stephansplatz, Herrengasse)

## The Jews of Vienna

Historically, Vienna has had an ambivalent relationship with its Jewish population, who first settled in the city in 1194.

In 1420 the Habsburg ruler Albrecht V issued a pogrom against the Jews, who later returned and prospered until the arrival of bigoted Leopold I and his even more bigoted wife, Margarita Teresa. In 1670, Jews were expelled from the city but were later invited back.

The following centuries saw Jews thrive under relatively benign conditions until 12 March 1938 when the Nazis occupied Austria. Violence exploded on the night of 9 November 1938 with the November Pogrom, when synagogues and prayer houses were burned – the **Stadttempel** (Map p62, C2; 01-531 04-0; www.ikg-wien.at; 01, Seitenstettengasse 4; tours adult/child €5/free; guided tours 11.30am & 2pm Mon-Thu Apr-Oct, 11.30am Mon-Thu Nov-Mar; 1, 2 Schwedenplatz, U Schwedenplatz) was the sole surviving synagogue – and 6500 Jews were arrested. Of the 180,000 Jews living in Vienna before the *Anschluss* (annexation), more than 100,000 managed to emigrate before the borders were closed in May 1939; another 65,000 died in ghettos or concentration camps: the steel-and-concrete **Holocaust-Denkmal** (Map p62, A2; 01, Judenplatz; U Stephansplatz) is a memorial to those who perished. Only 6000 survived to see the liberation by Allied troops in 1945.

Most survivors left afterwards. Today the city's Jewish population is approximately 7000.

# Eating

## Wrenkh

BISTRO **€€**

6 MAP P62, B4

Wrenkh specialises in vegetables, like lentils in white-wine sauce with bread dumplings, roast sweet potato stuffed with goat's cheese, and pumpkin soufflé with pistachio pesto. It also creates some superb fish-based dishes (grilled mountain-stream trout with smoked-garlic potato salad) and meat options (dry-aged rib-eye with miso and aubergine crème). On weekdays bargain-priced 2-/3-course lunch menus cost €10.50/11.50. (01-533 15 26; www.wrenkh-wien.at; 01, Bauernmarkt 10; mains €11.50-30; 11am-10pm Mon-Sat; ; U Stephansplatz)

## Huth Gastwirtschaft

AUSTRIAN **€€**

7 MAP P62, C7

One of several local neo-*Beisln* in this under-the-radar part of Innere Stadt, Huth serves superb Viennese classics, such as *Wiener Schnitzel* (Viennese cutlet) with cranberry sauce and parsley potatoes, and *Selchfleisch* (smoked pork with sauerkraut), as well as desserts including *Topfenstrudel* (quark-filled strudel) in a high-ceilinged main dining room, vaulted brick cellar and a summer terrace. (01-513 56 44; www.zum-huth.at; 01, Schellinggasse 5; mains €12.90-18.90; noon-11pm; 2 Weihburggasse)

## Tian

GASTRONOMY **€€€**

8 MAP P62, C6

Christian Holper's chandelier-lit, lounge-style restaurant takes 100% vegetarian cuisine to Michelin-starred heights using regionally sourced produce, including from Tian's own garden. Menus are zero choice, but might feature tomato and white-raspberry soup, porcini risotto with spruce shoots, and green-almond quinoa with broccoli. Wine pairings are available. Book well ahead. (01-890 46 65; www.tian-restaurant.com; 01, Himmelpfortgasse 23; 4-/6-/8-course lunch menus €89/109/127, 8-course dinner menu €127; 6-9pm Tue, noon-2pm & 6-9pm Wed-Sat; ; 2 Weihburggasse, U Stephansplatz)

## Motto am Fluss

INTERNATIONAL **€€**

9 MAP P62, D2

Located inside the Wien-City ferry terminal, with dazzling views of the Danube Canal, Motto am Fluss serves Austro–international cuisine with quality organic meats, fish (such as Donau trout) and vegetarian and vegan options. Its upstairs cafe does great all-day breakfasts, cakes and pastries, and its bar is a superbly relaxed hangout for Austrian wines, beers and house-creation cocktails. (01-252 55 10; www.mottoamfluss.at; 01, Franz-Josefs-Kai 2; restaurant mains €12.50-29, cafe dishes €5-12.50; restaurant 11.30am-2pm &

ANNA LURYE/SHUTTERSTOCK ©

Ankeruhr (p64)

6-11.30pm Mon-Fri, 6-11.30pm Sat & Sun, cafe 8am-midnight daily, bar 6pm-4am daily; ; 1, 2 Schwedenplatz, U Schwedenplatz)

### Griechenbeisl AUSTRIAN €€

10 MAP P62, D3

Dating from 1447 and frequented by Beethoven, Brahms, Schubert and Strauss among other luminaries, Vienna's oldest restaurant has vaulted rooms, wooden panelling and a plant-fringed front garden that's lovely in summer. Every classic Viennese dish is on the menu, along with three daily vegetarian options. (01-533 19 77; www.griechenbeisl.at; 01, Fleischmarkt 11; mains €17-29; 11.30am-11.30pm; ; 1, 2 Schwedenplatz, U Schwedenplatz)

## Drinking

### Kruger's American Bar BAR

11 MAP P62, B7

Retaining original decor from the 1920s and '30s, this dimly lit, wood-panelled American-style bar is a legend in Vienna, furnished with leather Chesterfield sofas and playing a soundtrack of Frank Sinatra, Dean Martin *et al* along with contemporary jazz. Cocktails, including highballs, fizzes, daiquiris and Collinses come in classic versions as well as creative spin-offs, such as Pisco Collins and lychee daiquiri. (www.krugers.at; 01, Krugerstrasse 5; 6pm-3am Mon-Thu, to 4am Fri & Sat, 7pm-2am Sun; D, 1, 2, 71 Kärntner Ring/Oper, U Stephansplatz)

### Zwölf Apostelkeller PUB

12 MAP P62, C4

Occupying a vast, dimly lit tri-level cellar dating back to the Romanesque and Gothic period, Zwölf Apostelkeller has a spirited atmosphere bolstered by traditional *Heuriger* (wine-taverns) ballads from 7pm daily. In addition to outstanding local wines, there's also a good choice of schnapps and beer, and a menu of traditional dishes, such as schnitzel, suckling pig and *Tafelspitz*, made from all-Austrian ingredients. (Twelve Apostle Cellar; 01-512 67 77; www.zwoelf-apostelkeller.at; 01, Sonnenfelsgasse 3; 11am-midnight; U Stephansplatz)

### Viennese Honey

Some 5000 bee colonies and 600 beekeepers harvest honey within Vienna's city limits, including on the rooftops of the Rathaus, Staatsoper, Kunsthistorisches Museum Vienna, Secession and several hotels. The fruits of their labour are sold at specialist honey boutique **Wald & Wiese** (Map p62, D4; www.waldundwiese.at; 01, Wollzeile 19; 10am-6.30pm Mon-Fri, to 5pm Sat; U Stephansplatz), which also sells honey-based beverages including mead, honey-and-whisky liqueur and grappa, along with beeswax candles, hand creams, toothpaste, royal jelly...

### 1516 Brewing Company MICROBREWERY

13 MAP P62, B8

Copper vats and brick walls give this locally loved venue an industrial look. It brews beers from malted wheat, rye and rice. The awning-shaded terrace gets packed in summer. Arrive early for a good seat when it screens international football games. (www.1516brewingcompany.com; 01, Schwarzenbergstrasse 2; 10am-2am; 2 Schwarzenbergstrasse, U Karlsplatz)

### Diglas CAFE

14 MAP P62, C4

Classic coffee house Diglas has crimson booths, timber-panelled walls with black-and-white photographs, vaulted ceilings, an extensive range of coffee and an elegant, venerable clientele. The reputation of Diglas' cakes precedes it, and the *Apfelstrudel* is unrivalled, as are the seasonal apricot or plum dumplings. Live piano music fills the room from 7pm. (01-512 57 65; www.diglas.at; 01, Wollzeile 10; 8am-10.30pm Mon-Fri, 9am-10.30pm Sat & Sun; U Stephansplatz)

## Entertainment

### Jazzland LIVE MUSIC

15 MAP P62, C2

Buried in a 500-year-old cellar beneath **Ruprechtskirche** (St Rupert's Church; 01-535 60 03; www.ruprechtskirche.at; 01, Ruprechtsplatz 1; 10am-noon Mon & Tue, 10am-noon & 3-5pm Wed, 10am-5pm Thu &

Fri, 11.30am-3.30pm Sat), Jazzland is Vienna's oldest jazz club, dating from 1972. The music covers the whole jazz spectrum, and features both local and international acts. Arrive early as it doesn't take reservations. (☎ 01-533 25 75; www.jazzland.at; 01, Franz-Josefs-Kai 29; cover €11-20; ⏰ 7pm-1am Mon-Sat mid-Aug–mid-Jul, live music from 9pm; 🚋 1, 2, 31 Schwedenplatz, U Schwedenplatz)

## Shopping

### So Austria

DESIGN

16 MAP P62, C3

Founded by two South Tyroleans with a passion for Austrian home and fashion accessories, this high-quality shop only sells goods handcrafted in Austria, including hand towels, tea towels, bags, shoes, jewellery, sculptures, hats, scarves and clothing. (www.so-austria.at; 01, Lugeck 3a; ⏰ 10am-7pm Mon-Fri, to 6pm Sat; U Stephansplatz)

### Vom Fass

FOOD & DRINKS

17 MAP P62, B4

The Austrian specialities that fill the shelves of this gourmet shop include Styrian pumpkin-seed oil, blueberry balsamic vinegar, Alpine herbal liqueurs from Tyrol, spiced walnut liqueur from Upper Austria, and smoked salt from Salzkammergut, as well as wines from around the country. Its website has recipes that incorporate the products. (www.vomfass-wien.at; 01, Brandstätte 5; ⏰ 10am-6.30pm Mon-Fri, to 6pm Sat; U Stephansplatz)

KARL ALLEN LUGMAYER/SHUTTERSTOCK ©

Walking Tour

# Stroll from Brunnenmarkt to Yppenplatz

*This morning stroll dipping into Vienna's 16th district, Ottakring, takes you for a ramble around the city's liveliest and longest street market, Brunnenmarkt. This edgy, ethnically diverse neighbourhood is now firmly on the city's hipster radar. Discover its independent boutiques, delis and cafes and get to know the new Vienna.*

## Getting There

Brunnenmarkt is about 2.5km west of the Hofburg.

2 to Neulerchenfelder Strasse

U Josefstädter Strasse

**Length** 700m; two hours

## ❶ Street Market

Begin Saturday Viennese-style with a mooch around **Brunnenmarkt** (16, Brunnengasse; 6am-6.30pm Mon-Fri, to 5pm Sat). Haphazard mountains of fabrics, clothing, fruit and veg, spices and coffee, cheese and meat – this market has the lot. Most stall owners are Turkish or Balkan, and Brunnengasse itself is lined with grocery stores, cafes and bakeries, where you can find authentic *pide* (Turkish pizza), flatbread, halva and baklava.

## ❷ Brunch Break

You could live in Vienna for a year and happily have a new lunchtime favourite every day in Yppenplatz. A long-standing favourite in the area is **Kent** (01-405 91 73; www.kentrestaurant.at; 16, Brunnengasse 67; breakfasts €5-10, mains €8-13.50; 6am-2am; ), a Turkish joint with a pretty tree-shaded garden for summertime snacking.

## ❸ Farm Fresh

The delis and boutiques on tree-dotted Yppenplatz are open most days, but the square is at its bustling best at the **Bauernmarkt** (16, Yppenplatz; 8am-1pm Fri & Sat), when farmers from Vienna's rural fringes sell their fruit, vegetables, meat, honey, preserves, wine and dairy goods. In summer the cafe crowds spill out onto pavement terraces and the square fills with chatter and street entertainers.

## ❹ Deli Delight

Deli **La Salvia** (01-236 72 27; www.lasalvia.at; 16, Yppenplatz; antipasti plates €7-10, pasta €9-12; 4-10pm Tue-Thu, from 10am Fri, 9am-3pm Sat) attracts gourmands with its picnic antipasti and stock of brilliant Italian wines, Prosecco, oils and *dolci* (sweets), as well as specialities like wild-boar salami. Taste its wares and revive over a perfectly made cappuccino or Aperol spritz in the bistro-cafe, or stay for lunch.

## ❺ Design District

Young designers and makers have set up shop on Yppenplatz, with a growing crop of cool boutiques and seasonal pop-ups adding to the market mix. A comparative old-timer, **Staud's** (www.stauds.com; 16, Yppenplatz; 8am-12.30pm & 3-6pm Tue-Fri, 8am-1pm Sat) is the go-to place in Vienna for sweet and savoury preserves that make great gifts.

# Explore Museum District & Neubau

*Showstopping attractions here include the incomparable Kunsthistorisches Museum Vienna, packed with old masters; the MuseumsQuartier's cache of museums, cafes, restaurants, bars and performance spaces; and the Burgtheater, where premieres have included works by Mozart and Beethoven. Neubau is an incubator for Vienna's vibrant fashion, art and design scenes.*

## The Short List

- ***Kunsthistorisches Museum Vienna (p74)*** *Exploring a whirl of Habsburg treasures from Egyptian tombs to artistic masterworks.*
- ***MuseumsQuartier (p80)*** *Visiting this vast ensemble of museums, cafes, restaurants and bars.*
- ***Naturhistorisches Museum (p84)*** *Encountering the dinosaurs and prehistoric divas.*
- ***Rathaus (p90)*** *Revelling in the neo-Gothic riches of the City Hall on a free guided tour.*
- ***Burgtheater (p90)*** *Taking a behind-the-scenes tour of Vienna's magnificent theatre.*

## Getting There & Around

U Useful U-Bahn stops include Museumsquartier (U2 line) and Volkstheater (U2 and U3). The U3 Neubaugasse and Zieglergasse stops, and the U6 stops Burggasse Stadthalle and Thaliastrasse are best for accessing Neubau.

Trams D, 1 and 71 travel around the Ringstrasse. The No. 49 line trundles from Ring/Volkstheater through Neubau.

**Museum District & Neubau Map on p88**

**Kunsthistorisches Museum (p74)** CANADASTOCK/SHUTTERSTOCK ©

Top Experience

# Revisit the Past at Kunsthistorisches Museum Vienna

*The Habsburgs built many bombastic palaces but the Kunsthistorisches Museum Vienna (KHM, Museum of Art History) is their magnum opus. Occupying a sumptuous neoclassical building, the museum takes you on an international treasure hunt. If your time's limited, skip straight to the Old Masters in the Picture Gallery.*

MAP P88, H4

www.khm.at

01, Maria-Theresien-Platz

adult/child incl Neue Burg museums €16/free

U Museumsquartier, Volkstheater

## Main Entrance

As you climb the ornate main staircase of the Kunsthistorisches Museum Vienna, your gaze is drawn to the ever-decreasing circles of the cupola, and marble columns guide the eye to delicately frescoed vaults, roaring lions and Antonio Canova's mighty statue of *Theseus Defeats the Centaur* (1805). Austrian legends Hans Makart and the brothers Klimt have left their hallmark between the columns and above the arcades – the former with lunette paintings, the latter with gold-kissed depictions of women inspired by Greco-Roman and Egyptian art.

## Picture Gallery

The museum's vast Gemäldegalerie (Picture Gallery) is by far and away the most impressive of its collections. Devote at least an hour or two to exploring its feast of Old Masters.

### Dutch, Flemish & German Painting

First up is the **German Renaissance**, where Lucas Cranach the Elder stages an appearance with engaging Genesis tableaux like *Paradise* (1530) and *Fall of Man* (aka *Adam and Eve;* 1537). The key focus, though, is the prized Dürer collection. Dürer's powerful compositions, sophisticated use of light and deep feeling for his subjects shine through in masterful pieces like *Portrait of a Venetian Lady* (1505), the spirit-soaring *Adoration of the Trinity* (1511) and the macabre *Martyrdom of the Ten Thousand* (1508).

Rubens throws you in the deep end of **Flemish baroque** painting next, with paintings rich in Counter-Reformation themes and mythological symbolism. The monumental *Miracles of St Francis Xavier* (1617), which used to hang in Antwerp's Jesuit church, the celestial *The Annunciation* (1610), the *Miracles of St Ignatius* (1615–20) and the *Triptych of St Ildefonso* (1630) all reveal the iridescent quality and linear clarity that underscored Rubens' style.

### ★ Top Tips

- Pick up an audio guide and a floor plan in the entrance hall to orientate yourself.
- Skip the queues by booking your ticket online.
- Opening hours are: 10am-6pm Fridays to Wednesdays and 10am-9pm on Thursdays from June to August. Visit 6-9pm on Thursdays for smaller crowds. It is closed on Mondays from September to May.
- Flash photography is not permitted.

### Take a Break

Hidden bistro-pub **Amerlingbeisl** (☎01-526 16 60; www.amerlingbeisl.at; 07, Stiftgasse 8; mains €8-16; ⏰kitchen noon-10pm, bar 11.30am-2am Mon-Fri, 10am-2am Sat & Sun; 🚋49 Siebensterngasse) has a charming vine-draped courtyard and seasonal Austrian cuisine.

Stop by **Saigon** (☎01-585 63 95; www.saigon.at; 06, Getreidemarkt 7; mains €9-19.50; ⏰11.30am-10.30pm; U Karlsplatz) for a steaming bowl of *phở*.

Mythological masterworks move from the gory, snake-riddled *Medusa* (1617) to the ecstatic celebration of love in *Feast of Venus* (1636).

In 16th- and 17th-century **Dutch Golden Age** paintings, the desire to faithfully represent reality through an attentive eye for detail and compositional *chiaroscuro* is captured effortlessly in works by Rembrandt, Ruisdael and Vermeer. Rembrandt's perspicuous *Self-Portrait* (1652), showing the artist in a humble painter's smock, Ruisdael's palpable vision of nature in *The Large Forest* (1655) and Vermeer's seductively allegorical *The Art of Painting* (1665), showing Clio, Greek muse of history, in the diffused light of an artist's studio, are all emblematic of the age.

Keenly felt devotional works by Flemish baroque master **Van Dyck** include *The Vision of the Blessed Hermann Joseph* (1630), in room 23, in which the Virgin and kneeling monk are bathed in radiant light, and *Virgin and Child with Saints Rosalie, Peter and Paul* (1629), in room XIV. An entire room (X) is given over to the vivid depictions of Flemish life and landscapes by Flemish Renaissance painter **Pieter Bruegel the Elder**, alongside his biblical star attraction, *The Tower of Babel* (1563).

### Italian, Spanish & French Painting

The first three rooms are given over to key exponents of the **16th-century Venetian** style: Titian, Veronese and Tintoretto. High on your artistic agenda here should be Titian's *Nymph and Shepherd* (1570), elevating the pastoral to the mythological in its portrayal of the futile desire of the flute-playing shepherd for the beautiful maiden out of his reach. Veronese's dramatic depiction of the suicidal Roman heroine *Lucretia* (1583), with a dagger drawn to her chest, and Tintoretto's *Susanna and the Elders* (1556), watched by two lustful power brokers, are also highlights.

Devotion is central to Raphael's *Madonna of the Meadow* (1506) in room III, one of the true masterpieces of the **High Renaissance**, as it is to the *Madonna of the Rosary* (1607), a stirring Counter-Reformation altarpiece by **Italian baroque** artist Caravaggio in room V. Room 7 is also a delight, with compelling works like Giuseppe Arcimboldo's anthropomorphic paintings inspired by the seasons and elements, such as fruit-filled *Summer* (1563), *Winter* (1563) and *Fire* (1566). Look out, too, for Venetian landscape painter Canaletto's *Schönbrunn* (1761), meticulously capturing the palace back in its imperial heyday.

Of the artists represented in the rooms dedicated to **Spanish, French and English** painting, the undoubted star is Spanish court-painter Velázquez. Particularly entrancing is his almost 3D portrait of *Infanta Margarita Teresa in a Blue Dress* (1651–73), in room 12, a vision of voluminous silk and eight-year-old innocence. English painter Sir Joshua Reynolds' studied *Portrait of a Young Lady* (c 1760–5), and French painter Jean-Marc Nattier the Younger's *Princess Maria Isabella of Parma* (1758) are both in room 13.

# Kunsthistoriches Museum Vienna

## First Floor: Gemäldegalerie (Picture Gallery)

## Ground Floor

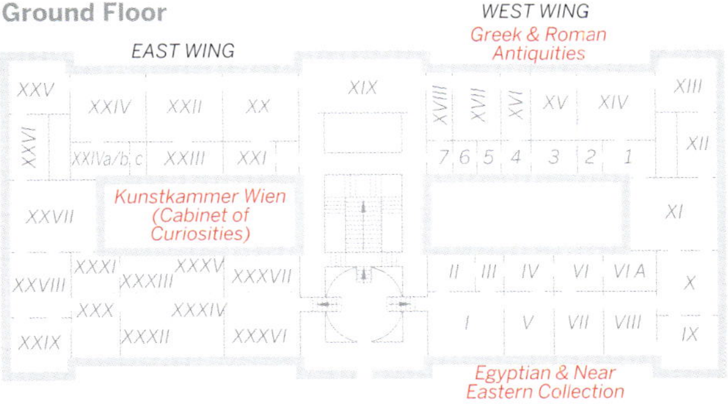

## Kunstkammer

Imagine the treasures you could buy with brimming coffers and the world at your fingertips. The Habsburgs did just that, filling their *Kunstkammer* (cabinet of art and curiosities) with an encyclopaedic collection of the rare and the precious: from narwhal-tusk cups to table holders encrusted with fossilised shark teeth. Its 20 themed rooms containing 2200 artworks open a fascinating window on the obsession with collecting curios in royal circles in Renaissance and baroque times.

The biggest crowd-puller here is Benvenuto Cellini's allegorical *Saliera* (salt cellar), room XXIX, commissioned by Francis I of France in 1540, which is exquisitely handcrafted from rolled gold, ivory and enamel. Among the Kunstkammer's other top-drawer attractions are the wildly expressive, early-17th-century ivory sculpture *Furie* (Master of the Furies), the serenely beautiful *Krumauer Madonna* (1400), a masterpiece of the Bohemian Gothic style, and Gasparo Miseroni's lapis lazuli *Dragon Cup* (1570), a fiery beast glittering with gemstones.

## Egyptian & Near Eastern Collection

Decipher the mysteries of Egyptian civilisations with a chronological romp through this miniature Giza of a ground-floor collection, beginning with predynastic and **Old Kingdom** treasures. Here the exceptionally well-preserved **Offering Chapel of Ka-ni-nisut** spells out the life of the high-ranking 5th-dynasty official in reliefs and hieroglyphs. The Egyptian fondness for adornment finds expression in artefacts such as a monkey-shaped kohl container and fish-shaped make-up palette.

Stele, sacrificial altar slabs, jewellery boxes, sphinx busts and pharaoh statues bring to life the **Middle Kingdom** and **New Kingdom**. The Egyptian talent for craftsmanship shines in pieces like a turquoise ceramic hippo (2000 BC) and the gold seal ring of Ramses X (1120 BC). The **Late Period** dips into the land of the pharaohs, at a time when their rule swung from Egypt to Persia. Scout out the 3000-year-old *Book of the Dead of Khonsu-mes*, the polychrome mummy board of Nes-pauti-taui and Canopic jars with lids shaped like monkey, falcon and jackal heads.

Stone sarcophagi, gilded mummy masks and busts of priests and princes transport you back to the **Ptolemaic** and **Greco-Roman** period. In the **Near Eastern** collection, the representation of a prowling lion from Babylon's triumphal Ishtar Gate (604–562 BC) is the big attraction.

## Greek & Roman Antiquities

This rich Greek and Roman repository reveals the imperial scope for collecting classical antiquities, with 2500 objects traversing three millennia from the Cypriot Bronze Age to early medieval times.

**Cypriot and Mycenaean Art** catapults you back to the dawn of Western civilisation, 2500 years ago. The big draw here is the precisely carved votive statue of a man wearing a finely pleated tunic. Among the muses, torsos and mythological statuettes in **Greek Art** is a fragment from the Parthenon's northern frieze showing two bearded men. The arts flourished in **Hellenistic** times, evident in exhibits like the *Amazonian Sarcophagus,* engraved with warriors so vivid you can almost hear their battle cries. In **pre-Roman Italy**, look for sculptures of Athena, funerary crowns intricately wrought from gold, and a repoussé showing the Titans doing battle with the gods.

The sizeable **Roman** stash includes the 4th-century AD *Theseus Mosaic* from Salzburg, a polychrome, geometric marvel recounting the legend of Theseus. You'll also want to take in the captivating 3rd-century AD *Lion Hunt* relief and the 1st-century AD *Gemma Augustea,* a sardonyx bas-relief cameo. Early medieval showstoppers include the shimmering golden vessels from the **Treasure of Nagyszentmiklós**, unearthed in 1799 in what is now Romania.

## Coin Collection

A piggy bank of gigantic Habsburg proportions, this coin collection covers three halls and three millennia on the 2nd floor (rooms I, II and III). The 2000 notes, coins and medallions on display are just a tiny fraction of the Kunsthistorisches Museum Vienna's 700,000-piece collection.

The coin collection's first hall presents medals of honour, first used in Renaissance Italy around 1400, and showcases gold and silver House of Habsburg wonders. The second hall travels through monetary time, from the birth of the coin in Lydia in the 7th century BC to the 20th century. Look out for classical coins, like the stater embellished with a lion head, in circulation under Alyattes, King of Lydia (610–560 BC), and Athenian coins featuring the goddess Athena and her owl symbol. The third hall stages one-off exhibitions.

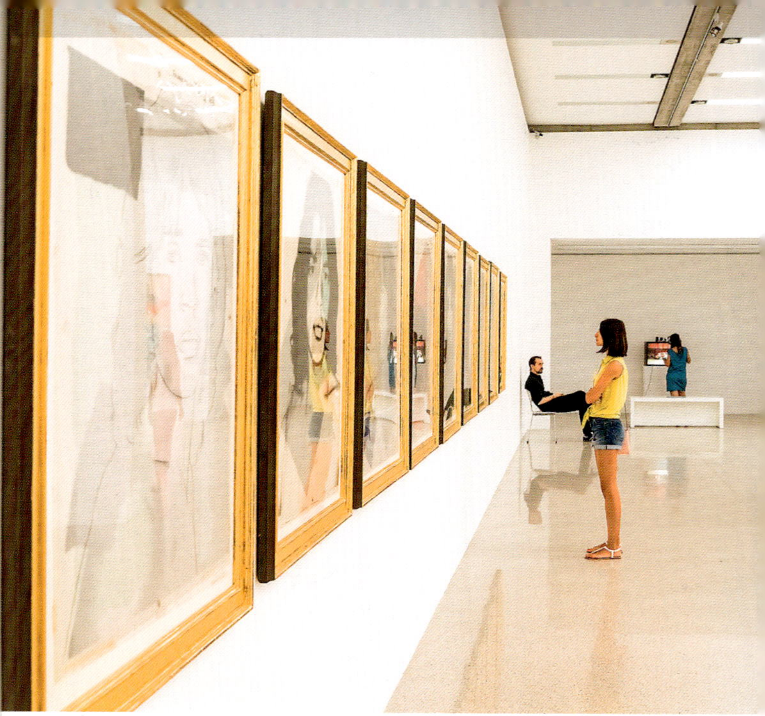

Top Experience

# Explore Past and Present at MuseumsQuartier

*Baroque heritage and the avant-garde collide at the MuseumsQuartier, one of the world's most-ambitious cultural spaces. Spanning 90,000 sq metres, this ensemble of museums, cafes, and performing-arts venues occupies the former imperial stables. You can't see it all in a day, so exploring selectively is the way to go.*

MAP P88, G4

Museum Quarter; MQ

01-523 58 81

www.mqw.at

07, Museumsplatz 1

49 Volkstheater

U Museumsquartier, Volkstheater

## Leopold Museum

The **Leopold Museum** (www.leopoldmuseum.org; adult/child €14/10; 10am-6pm Fri-Wed, to 9pm Thu Jun-Aug, closed Mon Sep-May) is named after Rudolf Leopold, a Viennese ophthalmologist who, on buying his first Egon Schiele (1890–1918) for a song as a young student in 1950, started to amass a huge private collection of mainly 19th-century and modernist Austrian artworks. In 1994 he sold the lot – 5266 paintings – to the Austrian government for €160 million (sold individually, the paintings would have made him €574 million), and the Leopold Museum was born. **Café Leopold** (www.cafeleopold.wien; 9.30am-midnight; ) is located on the top floor.

The Leopold has a white limestone exterior, open space (the 21m-high glass-covered atrium is lovely) and natural light flooding most rooms. Considering Rudolf Leopold's love of Schiele, it's no surprise the museum contains the world's largest collection of the painter's work: 41 paintings and 188 drawings and graphics. Among the standouts are the ghostly 1911 *Self-Seer II (Man and Death)*, the mournful *Mother with Two Children* (1915) and the 1912 caught-in-the-act *Cardinal and Nun (Caress)*.

Other artists well represented include Albin Egger-Lienz, with his unforgiving depictions of pastoral life, Richard Gerstl and Austria's third-greatest expressionist, Oskar Kokoschka. Of the handful of works on display by Klimt, the unmissable is the allegorical *Death and Life* (1910), a swirling amalgam of people juxtaposed by a skeletal grim reaper. Works by Adolf Loos, Josef Hoffmann and Otto Wagner are also on display.

## MUMOK

The dark basalt edifice and sharp corners of **MUMOK** (pictured; Museum Moderner Kunst, Museum of Modern Art; www.mumok.at; adult/child €12/free; 2-7pm Mon, 10am-7pm Tue, Wed & Fri-Sun, 10am-9pm Thu) are a complete contrast to the MQ's historical sleeve. Inside, MUMOK is crawling

### ★ Top Tips

- If you're planning on visiting several museums, combined tickets are available from the **MQ Point** (01-523 58 81; www.mqw.at; 10am-7pm).
- The **MQ Station Ticket** (€32) includes entry into every museum (Zoom only has a reduction) and a 30% discount on performances in the Tanzquartier Wien.
- The **MQ Type Ticket** (€26) gives admission into the Leopold Museum, MUMOK and Kunsthalle, and reduced entry into Zoom and the Tanzquartier Wien.

### Take a Break

Lounge on the terrace of the MuseumsQuartier's most relaxed cafe/bar, **Kantine** (01-523 82 39; www.mq-kantine.at; mains €9-13; kitchen 9am-11pm, bar to midnight; ).

with Vienna's finest collection of 20th- and 21st-century art, centred on Fluxus, nouveau realism, pop art and photorealism. The best of expressionism, cubism, minimal art and Viennese Actionism is represented in a collection of 9000 works that are rotated and exhibited by theme – but take note that sometimes all the Actionism is packed away to make room for temporary exhibitions. Viennese Actionism evolved in the 1960s as a radical leap away from mainstream art, in what some artists considered to be a restrictive cultural and political climate. Artists like Günter Brus, Hermann Nitsch and Rudolf Schwarzkogler aimed to shock with their violent, stomach-churning performance and action art, which often involved using the human body as a canvas. Not only did their work shock, some artists were even imprisoned for outraging public decency.

Other well-known artists represented throughout the museum – Pablo Picasso, Paul Klee, René Magritte, Max Ernst, Alberto Giacometti, Dorit Margreiter and Yto Barrada – are positively tame in comparison. Check the programme before visiting with children to ensure exhibits are suitable.

## Kunsthalle Wien

The **Kunsthalle** (Arts Hall; ☎01-521 890; www.kunsthallewien.at; adult/child €8/free; ⏰11am-7pm Tue, Wed & Fri-Sun, to 9pm Thu) is a collection of exhibition halls used to showcase local and international contemporary art. Its high ceilings, open planning and functionality have helped the venue leapfrog into the ranks of the top exhibition spaces in Europe. Programmes, which run for three to six months, rely heavily on photography, video, film, installations and new

### MuseumsQuartier Complex

media. Weekend visits include one-hour guided tours in English and German. The Saturday tours (Halle 1 at 3pm, Halle 2 at 4pm) focus on a theme, while Sunday tours (same times) give an overview.

## Architekturzentrum Wien

The **Architekturzentrum Wien** (Vienna Architecture Centre; 01-522 31 15; www.azw.at; adult/child €9/2.50; architecture centre 10am-7pm, library 10am-5.30pm Mon, Wed & Fri, to 7pm Sat & Sun) encompasses three halls used for temporary exhibitions, a library and a cafe. Exhibitions focus on international architectural developments and change on a regular basis. Check the online calendar and book ahead for regular walking tours through Vienna (in English and German) organised by the centre, covering various architectural themes.

## Zoom

Kids love this hands-on **children's museum** (01-524 79 08; www.kindermuseum.at; exhibition adult/child €6/free, activities child €5-7, accompanying adult €6; Tue-Sun; ), an arts-and-crafts session with lots of play thrown in. Budding Picassos have the chance to make, break, draw, explore and be creative in the 'Atelier'. 'Exhibition' stages a new exhibition every six months, while 'Ocean' appeals to tots with its mirrored tunnels, grottoes and ship deck for adventure play that stimulates coordination. For children aged eight to 14, there is an animated film studio and the future-focused Lab Club. Check schedules on the website. Activities last one to 1½ hours; reserve at the ticket office or online.

## Children's Theatre

**Dschungel Wien** (01-522 07 20 20; www.dschungelwien.at; tickets adult/child from €9/6; box office 4-6pm Mon-Fri; ) covers the entire spectrum, from drama and puppetry to music, dance and narrative theatre. There are generally several performances daily in German and occasionally in English; see the website for details. Adults pay children's prices for matinee performances.

## Dance

**Tanzquartier Wien** (01-581 35 91; www.tqw.at; tickets €10-57; box office 10am-4.30pm mid-Jul–Aug, 9am-7.30pm Mon-Fri, 10am-7.30pm Sat Sep–mid-Jul) is Vienna's first dance institution. It hosts an array of local and international performances with a strong experimental nature. Students receive a €10 discount on advance tickets. Unsold tickets (€5) go on sale 15 minutes before showtime.

## MuseumsQuartier Courtyards

The MuseumsQuartier's courtyards host a winter and summer programme of events, from film festivals to Christmas markets, literary readings to DJ nights; see the website www.mqw.at for details. They are also a popular hang-out in the summer months when the cafe terraces hum with life.

Top Experience

# Time Hop at Naturhistorisches Museum

*Vienna's astounding Naturhistorisches Museum (Museum of Natural History) covers four billion years of natural history in a blink. With its exquisitely stuccoed halls and eye-catching cupola, this late-19th-century building is the identical twin of the Kunsthistorisches Museum Vienna, which sits opposite. Among its minerals, fossils and dinosaur bones are one-of-a-kind archaeological finds.*

MAP P88, G3

www.nhm-wien.ac.at

01, Maria-Theresien-Platz

adult/child €12/free

9am-6.30pm Thu-Mon, to 9pm Wed

U Volkstheater

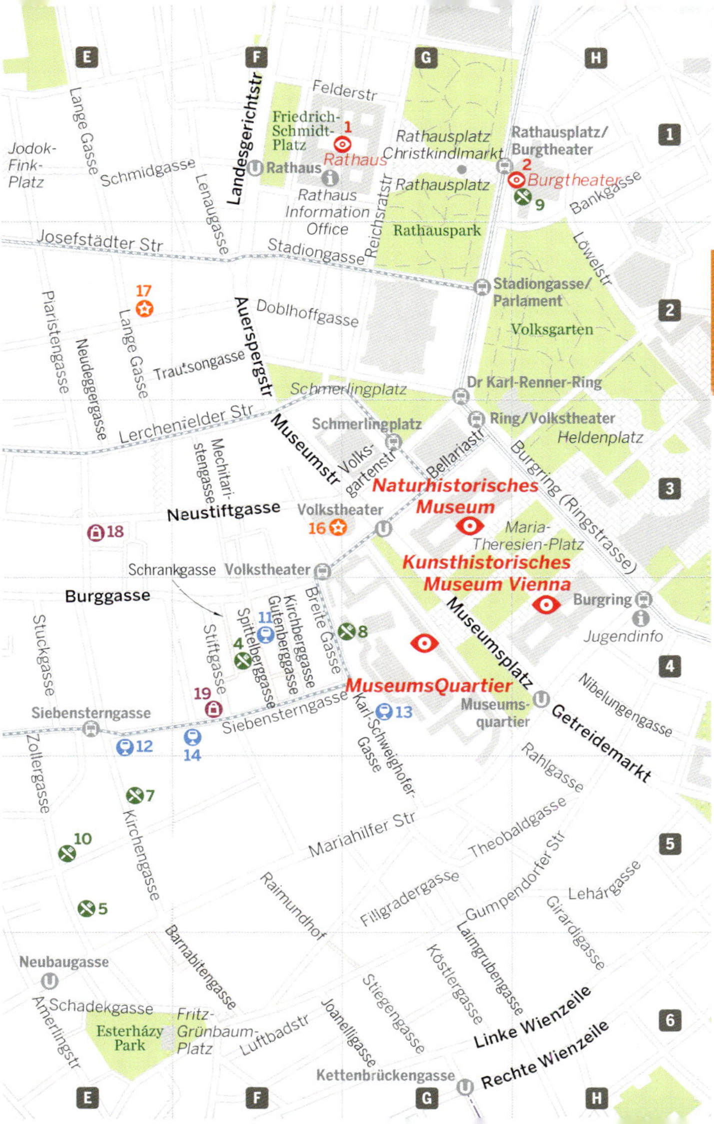
E
F
G
H
1
2
3
4
5
6
Felderstr
Landesgerichtstr
Friedrich-Schmidt-Platz
1
Rathaus
Rathaus
Rathaus Information Office
Rathausplatz Christkindlmarkt
Rathausplatz/ Burgtheater
2
Burgtheater
9
Rathausplatz
Rathauspark
Reichsratstr
Bankgasse
Jodok-Fink-Platz
Lange Gasse
Schmidgasse
Lenaugasse
Josefstädter Str
Stadiongasse
Löwelstr
Stadiongasse/ Parlament
Volksgarten
17
Piaristengasse
Neudeggergasse
Lange Gasse
Doblhoffgasse
Auerspergstr
Trautsongasse
Schmerlingplatz
Dr Karl-Renner-Ring
Ring/Volkstheater
Heldenplatz
Lerchenfelder Str
Mechitaristengasse
Museumstr
Schmerlingplatz
Volksgartenstr
Bellariastr
Burgring (Ringstrasse)
Naturhistorisches Museum
Neustiftgasse
Volkstheater
16
18
Maria-Theresien-Platz
Schrankgasse
Volkstheater
Kunsthistorisches Museum Vienna
Burggasse
Burgring
Museumsplatz
Jugendinfo
Stuckgasse
Stiftgasse
11
Spittelberggasse
Gutenberggasse
Kirchberggasse
Breite Gasse
8
4
MuseumsQuartier
Nibelungengasse
19
Siebensterngasse
Siebensterngasse
13
Museums-quartier
Getreidemarkt
Karl-Schweighofer-Gasse
Zollergasse
12
14
Rahlgasse
7
Kirchengasse
Mariahilfer Str
Theobaldgasse
10
Gumpendorfer Str
Lehárgasse
Raimundhof
Filigradergasse
5
Girardigasse
Laimgrubengasse
Barnabitengasse
Köstlergasse
Neubaugasse
Stiegengasse
Schadekgasse
Amerlingstr
Esterházy Park
Fritz-Grünbaum-Platz
Luftbadstr
Joanelligasse
Linke Wienzeile
Rechte Wienzeile
Kettenbrückengasse

# Sights

## Rathaus

HISTORIC BUILDING

1 MAP P88, G1

Vienna's neo-Gothic City Hall, completed in 1883 by Friedrich von Schmidt (who also designed Cologne Cathedral) and modelled on Flemish city halls, with lacy stonework, pointed-arch windows and spindly turrets, is the highlight of the Ringstrasse boulevard's 19th-century architectural ensemble. Bronze statues of Joseph Lanner and Johann Strauss I stand in the fountain-filled **Rathauspark**.

Free one-hour guided tours are in German; multilingual audio guides are also free. (City Hall; 01-502 55; www.wien.gv.at; 01, Rathausplatz 1; admission free; tours 1pm Mon, Wed & Fri Sep-Jun, 1pm Mon-Fri Jul & Aug; D, 1, 2, 71 Rathausplatz/Burgtheater, U Rathaus)

## Burgtheater

THEATRE

2 MAP P88, H1

This stately Renaissance-style **theatre** (National Theatre; 01-514 44 4140; www.burgtheater.at; 01, Universitätsring 2; seats €7-61, standing room €3.50; box office 9am-5pm Mon-Fri, closed Jul & Aug; D, 1, 71 Rathausplatz/Burgtheater) sits with aplomb on the Ringstrasse. Designed by Gottfried Semper and Karl von Hasenauer and completed in 1888, it was restored to its pre-WWII glory in 1955.

The theatre company dates to 1741, making it Europe's second oldest. If the walls could talk, they'd tell of musical milestones like the premiere of Mozart's *The Marriage of Figaro* (1786) and Beethoven's *First Symphony* (1800). For a behind-the-scenes look at this magnificent theatre, join a 50-minute guided tour. (01-514 44 4140; www.burgtheater.at; 01, Universitätsring 2; tours adult/child €7/3.50; English tours 3pm daily Jul & Aug, 3pm Fri-Sun Sep-Jun; D, 1, 71 Rathausplatz/Burgtheater)

## Hofmobiliendepot

MUSEUM

3 MAP P88, D6

The Habsburgs stashed away the furniture not displayed in the Hofburg, Schönbrunn, Schloss Belvedere and their other palaces at the Hofmobiliendepot. A romp through this regal attic of a museum, covering four floors and 165,000 objects, provides fascinating insight into furniture design, with highlights such as a display of imperial travelling thrones, Emperor Maximilian's coffin and Empress Elisabeth's neo-Renaissance bed from Gödöllő Castle.

One of the more underrated museums in the city, it's included in the Sisi Ticket (p46). (Imperial Furniture Collection; 01-524 33 57; www.hofmobiliendepot.at; 07, Andreasgasse 7; adult/child incl audio guide €10.50/6.50, incl 1hr guided tour €12.50/7.50; 10am-6pm Tue-Sun; U Zieglergasse)

# Eating

## Tian Bistro

VEGETARIAN €€

4 MAP P88, F4

Colourful tables are set up on the cobbled laneway outside Tian Bistro in summer, while indoors, a glass roof floods the atrium-style, greenery-filled dining room in light. It's the cheaper, more relaxed offspring of Michelin-starred vegetarian restaurant Tian (p66), and serves sensational vegetarian and vegan dishes, such as black-truffle risotto with Piedmont hazelnuts, as well as brunch until 1pm on weekends. (01-890 466 532; www.tian-bistro.com; 07, Schrankgasse 4; mains €9-18; 5.30-10pm Mon, noon-10pm Tue-Fri, 10am-10pm Sat & Sun; ; 49 Siebensterngasse)

## Liebling

CAFE €

5 MAP P88, E5

No sign hangs above the door at Liebling, whose distressed walls, stripped-back floorboards and mishmash of flea-market furniture create a cool, laid-back vibe. Settle in for breakfast (until 4pm) and lunch of wholesome daily specials like spinach-feta strudel or pumpkin and pine-nut wraps, topped off with chocolate-lavender cake. There are also freshly squeezed juices to enjoy throughout the day.

By night the bar is rocking. Cash only. (01-990 58 77; www.facebook.com/liebling1070; 07, Zollergasse 6; dishes €3.50-11; kitchen 9am-10pm daily, bar 9am-2am Mon-Thu, to 4am Fri & Sat, to midnight Sun; ; ; U Neubaugasse)

Ice skating on Rathausplatz

CREATIVEMARC/GETTY IMAGES ©

## Swing Kitchen

VEGAN €

6 MAP P88, C6

Eco-minded Swing Kitchen calculates that its all-organic vegan burgers use 93% less land, 85% less water, 96% less grain, 95% less energy and produce 92% less greenhouse emissions than meat-based burgers. Its four varieties include a vegan schnitzel Vienna burger and Swing Burger with smoky barbecue sauce. Fries and onion rings are cooked in vegetable oil; there are also salads. (www.swingkitchen.com; 07, Schottenfeldgasse 3; dishes €5-9; 11am-10pm; ; U Zieglergasse)

## Figar

CAFE €

7 MAP P88, E5

Splashed with a street-art-style mural, this neighbourhood favourite serves mighty breakfasts until 4pm, from Working Class Hero (sausage, mushrooms, home-made baked beans, spinach and skewered roast cherry tomatoes) to Exquisite (Viennese Thum ham, chorizo, Emmental and scrambled eggs), plus yoghurt, muesli, porridge and pastries.

At night it morphs into a craft cocktail bar with a soundtrack of house music. (01-890 99 47; http://1070.figar.net; 07, Kirchengasse 18; breakfast €4.50-9.50, mains €10-16; kitchen 8am-10.30pm Mon-Fri, 9am-10.30pm Sat & Sun, bar to midnight Sun-Wed, to 2am Thu-Sat; ; 49 Siebensterngasse, U Neubaugasse)

## Glacis Beisl

BISTRO €€

8 MAP P88, G4

Hidden downstairs along Breite Strasse in the MuseumsQuartier (follow the signs from MUMOK), Glacis Beisl does an authentic *Krautfleckerl* (cabbage-and-pasta bake), an accomplished *Wiener Schnitzel* (Viennese cutlet) and some other very decent Austrian classics, which you can wash down with Viennese whites and reds. In summer dine beneath the walnut trees among flowering geraniums in the sprawling courtyard. (01-526 56 60; www.glacisbeisl.at; 07, Breite Gasse 4; mains €8-21.50; kitchen noon-11pm, bar 11am-2am; ; 49 Volkstheater, U Volkstheater)

## Vestibül

AUSTRIAN €€€

9 MAP P88, H1

In the southern wing of the Burg-theater (p90), Vestibül is a showpiece of marble columns and stucco topped off with a glorious sparkling mirrored bar. The menu is a contemporary take on traditional cuisine with a strong regional and seasonal focus; expect such dishes as lobster meat with sauerkraut or braised veal shoulder with smoked catfish sauce. Reservations are recommended. (01-532 49 99; www.vestibuel.at; 01, Universitätsring 2; mains €18-31, 3-/4-course dinner menus €58/72; noon-2.30pm & 6-10.30pm Tue-Fri, 6-10.30pm Sat; D, 1, 71 Rathausplatz/Burgtheater)

### Tart'a Tata

PASTRIES €

10 MAP P88, E5

Exquisite French pastries – rainbows of macarons, glossy eclairs, *babas au rhum* (rum-soaked yeast cakes) and superb *tartes aux fraises* (strawberry tarts) – are laid out like jewels at this patisserie, which also makes flaky, buttery croissants and *pains au chocolat* (chocolate-filled glazed pastries). Pick up treats to take away or dine at its on-site cafe. (07, Lindengasse 35; pastries €1.20-5; 10am-6pm Mon-Sat; U Neubaugasse)

## Drinking

### Melete Art Design Cocktails

COCKTAIL BAR

11 MAP P88, F4

Both an art gallery and a hopping bar, Melete ingeniously pairs changing art exhibitions with inventive drinks. Its 'Africa' exhibition, for instance, featured cocktails like Madagascan Sunrise (vanilla-infused rum, hibiscus syrup and mango juice), while 'Art of Light' inspired concoctions such as Solar (yellow Chartreuse, gin, sweet vermouth and yuzu). Artworks exhibited are for sale; check the programme online. (www.melete.at; 07, Spittelberggasse 18; 5-10pm Thu & Fri, 3-10pm Sat; ; 49 Volkstheater)

### J Hornig Kaffeebar

COFFEE

12 MAP P88, E4

Farm-direct beans roasted on-site at this third-wave coffee specialist are utilised in espresso, pour over, Aeropress, ice-drip and cold-brew techniques to create a perfect cup, which you can pair with locally baked cakes. The state-of-the-art space has a stainless-steel ceiling, industrial fixtures and designer plywood chairs, and plenty of power sockets to recharge your devices. (www.jhornig.com; 07, Siebensterngasse 29; 7.30am-7pm Mon-Fri, 9am-7pm Sat & Sun; ; Siebensterngasse)

### Donau

CLUB

13 MAP P88, G4

DJs spin techno to a pumped crowd at this underground club with soaring columns, striking digital projections on the walls, and its own on-site *Würstelstand* (sausage stand). It's easily missed – look for the grey metal door. Hours can vary. (www.donautechno.com; 07, Karl-Schweighofer-Gasse 10; 8pm-4am Mon-Thu, to 6am Fri & Sat, to 2am Sun; U Museumsquartier)

### Siebensternbräu

MICROBREWERY

14 MAP P88, F4

Taste some of Vienna's finest microbrews at this lively, no-nonsense brewpub. Besides hoppy lagers and malty ales, there are unusual varieties like chilli or wood-smoked beer. Try them with pretzels or pub grub like *Schnitzel*, goulash and pork knuckles (lunch mains €6.90, dinner mains €7.90 to €18.90). The courtyard garden fills up quickly in the warmer months. (www.7stern.at; 07, Siebensterngasse 19; 11am-midnight; ; 49 Siebensterngasse)

### Wirr

BAR, CLUB

15 MAP P88, D4

On weekends it's often hard to find a seat on the time-worn sofas at this colourful, alternative bar with walls covered in works by local artists. In the cellar, **Dual** (www.clubdual.at) hosts electro clubbing events. (www.wirr.at; 07, Burggasse 70; 8am-2am Sun-Wed, to 4am Thu-Sat; 46 Strozzigasse)

## Entertainment

### Volkstheater

THEATRE

16 MAP P88, F3

With a seating capacity close to 1000, the Volkstheater is one of Vienna's largest theatres. Built in 1889, the interior is suitably grand. While most performances are of translated works (anything from Ingmar Bergman to Molière), only German-language shows are staged. Advance bookings are necessary; students can buy unsold tickets for €5 one hour before performances start. (01-521 11-400; www.volkstheater.at; 07, Arthur-Schnitzler-Platz 1; tickets €9-55; box office 10am-7.30pm Mon-Sat; U Volkstheater)

### Vienna's English Theatre

THEATRE

17 MAP P88, E2

Founded in 1963, Vienna's English Theatre is the oldest foreign-language theatre in Vienna (with the occasional show in French or Italian). Productions range from timeless pieces, such as Shakespeare, to contemporary works

Rathausplatz Christkindlmarkt

ROBERTO MOIOLA/SYSAWORLD/GETTY IMAGES ©

## Christmas Markets

Vienna's much-loved Christmas market season runs from around mid-November to Christmas Eve. Magical *Christkindlmärkte* set up in streets and squares, with stalls selling wooden toys, holiday decorations and traditional food such as *Wurst* (sausages) and *Glühwein* (mulled wine). The centrepiece is the **Rathausplatz Christkindlmarkt** (www.wienerweihnachtstraum.at; 01, Rathausplatz; mid-Nov–26 Dec; D, 1, 71 Rathausplatz/Burgtheater, U Rathaus).

Spread over the charming cobbled streets of the Spittelberg quarter, the charming **Spittelberg Christkindlmarkt** (www.spittelberg.at; 07, Spittelberggasse; mid-Nov–23 Dec; U Volkstheater, Museumsquartier) is traditionally the most beloved by the Viennese.

and comedies. Students receive a 20% discount and are eligible for standby tickets (€10), which go on sale 15 minutes before showtime. (01-402 12 60-0; www.englishtheatre.at; 08, Josefsgasse 12; tickets €24-47; box office 10am-7pm Mon-Fri, 5-7pm Sat performance days, closed Jul–mid-Aug; 2 Rathaus, U Rathaus)

# Shopping

### Runway — FASHION & ACCESSORIES

18 MAP P88, E3

Runway is a launching pad for up-and-coming Austrian fashion designers, whose creations sit alongside those of their established compatriots. Framed by arched windows, the whitewashed space showcases the direction of Viennese womenswear today through its rotating racks of clothes and accessories. (www.runwayvienna.at; 07, Kirchengasse 48; 11am-12.30pm & 1-6.30pm Tue-Fri, to 6pm Sat; 46 Strozzigasse)

### Schokov — CHOCOLATE

19 MAP P88, F4

Thomas Kovazh turned his chocolate-making dream into reality when he opened this sleek gallery-style shop. Today, Schokov sells some of Vienna's best pralines and truffles (over 200 varieties). Chilli, lavender, sea-salt, potato and pepper chocolate – you'll find them all in bar form here, alongside top Austrian brands like Zotter and Scharffen Berger. A 1½-hour, 20-chocolate-tasting workshop (English available) costs €29. (www.schokov.com; 07, Siebensterngasse 20; noon-6.30pm Mon-Fri, 10am-6pm Sat; 49 Siebensterngasse)

KARLSPLATZ

Explore

# Karlsplatz

*Fringing the Ringstrasse in the southeast corner of the Innere Stadt, this neighbourhood includes the city's sublime Staatsoper opera house, and extends south beyond Vienna's enormous market and food paradise, the Naschmarkt, into some of the city's most interesting* Vorstädte *(inner suburbs): Margareten, Mariahilf and Wieden. There's great eating, drinking and nightlife, and a truly Viennese* Vorstadt *character.*

## The Short List

- ***Staatsoper (p98)*** *Reliving operatic highs on a guided tour of this resplendent opera house.*
- ***Karlskirche (p104)*** *Catching the lift up to this church's dome to view its incredible frescoes.*
- ***Secession (p104)*** *Contemplating Klimt's Beethoven Frieze and other works by Vienna Secession–movement artists.*
- ***Naschmarkt (p111)*** *Breathing in the market's heady aromas of spices, olives, oils, vinegars, cheeses, hams, sausages and more.*
- ***Akademie der Bildenden Künste (p104)*** *Viewing Bosch's riveting triptych,* The Last Judgment *altarpiece.*

## Getting There & Around

U Karlsplatz is well connected to all corners of Vienna, served by the U-Bahn lines U1, U2 and U4.

Key routes include trams 1 and 62, which stop at Karlsplatz.

**Karlsplatz Map on p102**

GREGOR SCHUSTER/GETTY IMAGES ©

Top Experience

# Raise the curtain on the Staatsoper

*Built between 1861 and 1869 by August Sicard von Sicardsburg and Eduard van der Nüll, Vienna's foremost opera and ballet venue initially revolted the city's public and Habsburg royalty and quickly earned the nickname 'stone turtle'. Despite the frosty reception, the Staatsoper went on to house some of the most iconic directors in history, including Gustav Mahler, Richard Strauss and Herbert von Karajan.*

MAP P102, G1

www.wiener-staatsoper.at

01, Opernring 2

D, 1, 2, 62, 71 Kärntner Ring/Oper,

U Karlsplatz

## Guided Tours

Guided tours take in highlights such as the foyer, graced with busts of Beethoven, Schubert and Haydn and frescoes of celebrated operas, and the main staircase, watched over by marble allegorical statues embodying the liberal arts. The Tea Salon dazzles in 22-carat gold leaf, the Schwind Foyer captivates with 16 opera-themed oil paintings by Austrian artist Moritz von Schwind, while the Gustav Mahler Hall is hung with tapestries inspired by Mozart's *The Magic Flute*.

You'll also get a behind-the-scenes look at the stage, which raises the curtain on over 300 performances each year.

## Performances

Productions are lavish, formal affairs, where people dress up accordingly. In the interval, wander the foyer and refreshment rooms to fully appreciate the gold-and-crystal interior.

**Tickets** (☎01-514 44 7880; www.bundes98theater.at; 01, Operngasse 2; ⌚8am-6pm Mon-Fri, 9am-noon Sat & Sun; U Stephansplatz) can be purchased up to two months in advance. Note that opera is not performed here in July and August (though tours still take place).

## Opernball

Of the 300-or-so Viennese balls held in January and February, the **Opernball** (www.wiener-staatsoper.at) is number one. Held in the Staatsoper on the Thursday preceding Ash Wednesday, it's a supremely lavish affair, with the men in tails and women in shining white gowns.

Tickets range from €315 to an eye-watering €23,600 and sell out years in advance.

### ★ Top Tips

- Guided tours (adult/child €9/4) in English and German last 40 minutes. The tours generally depart on the hour between 10am and 4pm.
- Portraits of operatic greats, costumes, stage designs and documents are displayed in the **TheaterMuseum** (☎01-525 24 3460; www.theatermuseum.at; 01, Lobkowitzplatz 2; adult/child incl all exhibitions €12/free; ⌚10am-6pm Wed-Mon; 🚋D, 1, 2, 62, 71 Kärntner Ring/Oper, U Stephansplatz), located near the Hofburg.

### ✕ Take a Break

Retaining its 1920s *Jugendstil* decor, **Café Tirolerhof** (www.facebook.com/pg/cafetirolerhof; 01, Führichgasse 8; ⌚7am-10pm Mon-Sat, 9.30am-8pm Sun; 📶; 🚋D, 1, 2, 71 Kärntner Ring/Oper, U Stephansplatz, Karlsplatz) makes an atmospheric stop for coffee and cake.



KONSTANTIN TRONIN/SHUTTERSTOCK ©

Walking Tour

# Epicurean Tour of the Freihausviertel

*Once home to impoverished artisans, the Freihausviertel has since been revitalised: its attractive lanes hold boho cafes, speciality food stores and some of Vienna's most exciting new galleries, ateliers and boutiques. After browsing Vienna's gourmand's fantasyland, the Naschmarkt, continue your spin through the district with this food-and-drink tour.*

## Walk Facts

**Start** Sekt Comptoir (U Kettenbrückengasse)

**End** Fruth U Kettenbrückengasse)

**Length** 1.4km; two hours

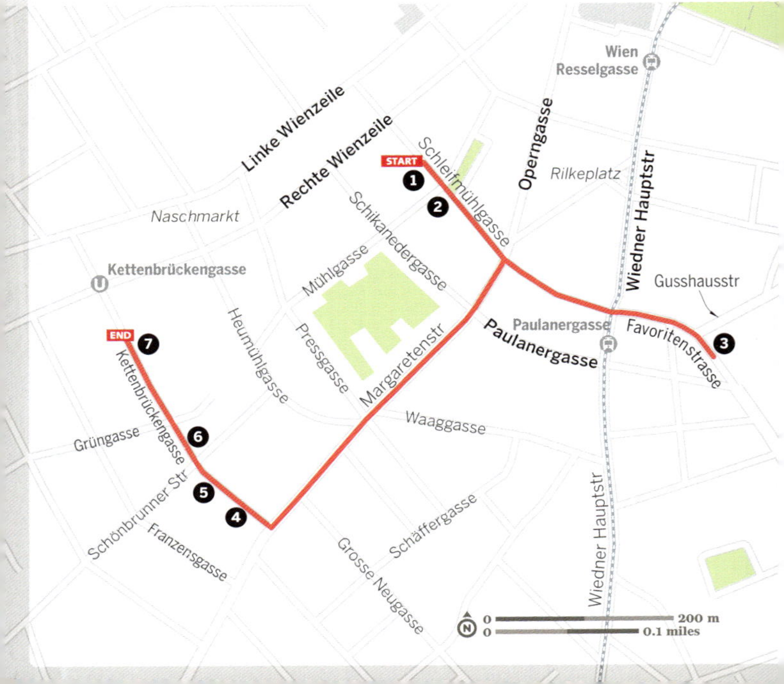

## ❶ Austrian Bubbly

Raise a toast at **Sekt Comptoir** (www.sektcomptoir.at; 04, Schleifmühl gasse 19; ⏰5-11pm Mon-Thu, 3-11pm Fri, noon-11pm Sat) over a glass of *Sekt* (sparkling wine) produced at its own vineyard. It's a great place to stock up on bottles, too.

## ❷ Literary Lunch

Not only can you browse cookbooks at **Babette's** (www.babettes.at; 04, Schleifmühlgasse 17; ⏰10am-7pm Mon-Fri, 10.30am-5pm Sat Sep-Jul, 11am-6pm Mon-Fri, 10am-3pm Sat Aug), but from noon to 2.30pm on weekdays you can taste international lunch specials prepared in its open kitchen with own-brand spices and fresh Naschmarkt produce.

## ❸ Cutting-Edge Coffee

Burgenland-roasted beans brewed to perfection using state-of-the-art espresso machines are the hallmark of contemporary, whitewashed cafe-shop **Kaffeefabrik** (www.kaffeefabrik.at; 04, Favoritenstrasse 4-6; ⏰8am-6pm Mon-Fri, 11am-5pm Sat).

## ❹ Sugar & Spice

At **Henzls Ernte** (www.henzls.at; 05, Kettenbrückengasse 3; ⏰1-6pm Tue-Fri, 9am-5pm Sat), you might see the Henzl family drying, grinding and blending their home-grown and foraged herbs and spices with sugar and salt. Specialities include sloe-berry salt, lavender sugar and wild-garlic pesto.

## ❺ Farm Produce

Nip into farmers' store **Helene** (www.bauernladenhelene.at; 05, Kettenbrückengasse 7; ⏰8am-6pm Tue-Fri, to 3pm Sat) for top-quality regional produce. Besides super-fresh fruit, veggies, cheese and meat, you'll find Joseph Brot vom Pheinsten organic loaves; chestnut, larch and acacia honeys; and wine and chilli jam.

## ❻ Regional Cheeses

All-organic Austrian cheeses made by small artisan dairies are the speciality of **Käseschatztruhe** (www.kaeseschatztruhe.at; 04, Kettenbrückengasse 10; ⏰10am-6.30pm Wed-Fri, 9am-2.30pm Sat). Varieties might include Froihof's soft sheep cheeses from Styria, Ziegenliese's semihard goat's cheeses from Burgenland, and Plangger's *Höhlentaler* (similar to Emmental) from Tyrol.

## ❼ Just Desserts

At chocolatier and patisserie **Fruth** (www.fruth.at; 04, Kettenbrückengasse 20; ⏰11am-7pm Tue-Fri, 9am-5pm Sat), Eduard Fruth creates edible works of art. Delicacies include strawberry tartlets, rich truffles, feather-light eclairs, and chocolate flavoured with chilli, chestnut and cranberry.

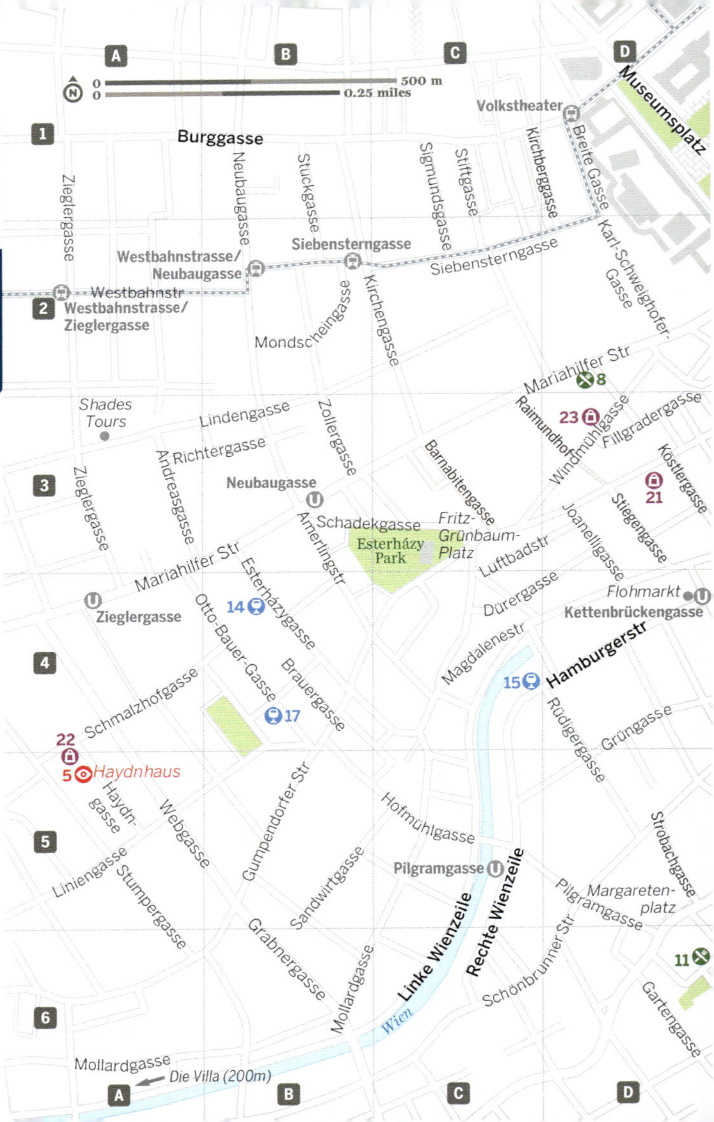
A
B
C
D
1
2
3
4
5
6
0 500 m
0 0.25 miles
Burggasse
Volkstheater
Museumsplatz
Breite Gasse
Kirchberggasse
Stiftgasse
Sigmundsgasse
Stuckgasse
Neubaugasse
Zieglergasse
Siebensterngasse
Westbahnstrasse/ Neubaugasse
Westbahnstr
Westbahnstrasse/ Zieglergasse
Karl-Schweighofer-Gasse
Mondscheingasse
Kirchengasse
Mariahilfer Str
8
Shades Tours
Lindengasse
Richtergasse
Zollergasse
Raimundhof
23
Windmühlgasse
Fillgradergasse
Köstlergasse
21
Barnabitengasse
Andreasgasse
Neubaugasse
Schadekgasse
Fritz-Grünbaum-Platz
Esterházy Park
Amerlingstr
Joanelligasse
Stiegengasse
Luftbadstr
Mariahilfer Str
Zieglergasse
14
Esterházygasse
Otto-Bauer-Gasse
Dürergasse
Flohmarkt
Kettenbrückengasse
Magdalenestr
Hamburgerstr
15
Brauergasse
17
Schmalzhofgasse
22
5 Haydnhaus
Haydngasse
Webgasse
Gumpendorfer Str
Rüdigergasse
Grüngasse
Hofmühlgasse
Strobachgasse
Liniengasse
Stumpergasse
Sandwirtgasse
Pilgramgasse
Linke Wienzeile
Rechte Wienzeile
Margareten-platz
Pilgramgasse
Grabnergasse
Mollardgasse
Schönbrunner Str
11
Gartengasse
Wien
Mollardgasse
Die Villa (200m)

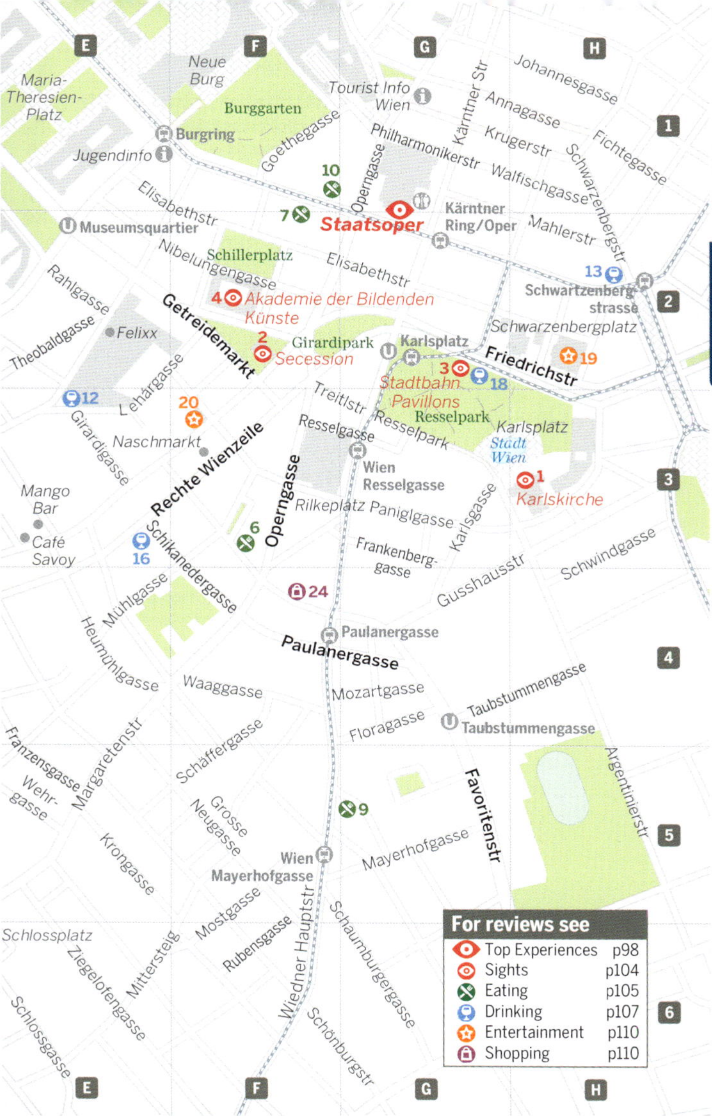
E
F
G
H
1
2
3
4
5
6
Maria-Theresien-Platz
Neue Burg
Burggarten
Tourist Info Wien
Burgring
Jugendinfo
Goethegasse
Johannesgasse
Annagasse
Kärntner Str
Krugerstr
Fichtegasse
Philharmonikerstr
Walfischgasse
Schwarzenbergstr
10
Operngasse
7
Staatsoper
Kärntner Ring/Oper
Mahlerstr
Elisabethstr
Museumsquartier
Nibelungengasse
Schillerplatz
13
Schwartzenbergstrasse
4 Akademie der Bildenden Künste
Rahlgasse
Getreidemarkt
Schwarzenbergplatz
Theobaldgasse
Felixx
2 Secession
Girardipark
Karlsplatz
Friedrichstr
19
3 Stadtbahn Pavillons
18
12
Lehárgasse
20
Treitlstr
Resselpark
Girardigasse
Naschmarkt
Resselgasse
Rechte Wienzeile
Karlsplatz
Stadt Wien
Wien Resselgasse
1 Karlskirche
Mango Bar
Café Savoy
16
Schikanedergasse
6
Operngasse
Rilkeplatz
Paniglgasse
Karlsgasse
Frankenberggasse
Schwindgasse
Gusshausstr
Mühlgasse
24
Heumühlgasse
Paulanergasse
Paulanergasse
Waaggasse
Mozartgasse
Taubstummengasse
Floragasse
Taubstummengasse
Franzensgasse
Margaretenstr
Schäffergasse
Wehrgasse
Favoritenstr
Argentinierstr
Grosse Neugasse
9
Krongasse
Wien Mayerhofgasse
Mayerhofgasse
Schlossplatz
Mostgasse
Wiedner Hauptstr
Schaumburgergasse
Rubensgasse
Mittersteig
Ziegelofengasse
Schlossgasse
Schönburgstr
For reviews see
Top Experiences p98
Sights p104
Eating p105
Drinking p107
Entertainment p110
Shopping p110

# Sights

## Karlskirche
CHURCH

1 MAP P102, H3

Built between 1716 and 1739, after a vow by Karl VI at the end of the 1713 plague, Vienna's finest baroque church rises at the southeast corner of Resselpark. It was designed and commenced by Johann Bernhard Fischer von Erlach and completed by his son Joseph. The huge elliptical copper dome reaches 72m; the highlight is the lift to the cupola (included in admission) for a close-up view of the intricate frescos by Johann Michael Rottmayr. (St Charles Church; www.karlskirche.at; 04, Karlsplatz; adult/child €8/4; 9am-6pm Mon-Sat, noon-7pm Sun; U Karlsplatz)

## Secession
MUSEUM

2 MAP P102, F2

In 1897, 19 progressive artists left the mainstream Künstlerhaus artistic establishment to form the *Wiener Secession* (Vienna Secession). Among their number were Gustav Klimt, Josef Hoffmann, Kolo Moser and Joseph Olbrich. Olbrich designed the new exhibition centre of the Secessionists, which combined sparse functionality with stylistic motifs. Its biggest draw is Klimt's exquisitely gilded *Beethoven Frieze*. One-hour guided tours in English (€3) take place at 11am on Saturdays. An audio guide costs €3. (www.secession.at; 01, Friedrichstrasse 12; adult/child €9.50/6; 10am-6pm Tue-Sun; U Karlsplatz)

## Stadtbahn Pavillons
HISTORIC BUILDING

3 MAP P102, G2

Peeking above the Resselpark at Karlsplatz are two of Otto Wagner's finest designs, the Stadtbahn Pavillons. Built in 1898 at a time when Wagner was assembling Vienna's first public transport system (1893–1902), the pavilions are gorgeous examples of *Jugendstil*, with floral motifs and gold trim on a steel and marble structure. The western pavilion holds an exhibit on Wagner's most famous *Jugendstil* works, the **Kirche am Steinhof** (www.erzdioezese-wien.at; 14, Baumgartner Höhe 1; tour €8; 4-5pm Sat, noon-4pm Sun, tours 3pm Sat, 4pm Sun; 48A Otto-Wagner-Spital) and Postsparkasse (p61). The eastern pavilion is home to Club U (p109). (www.wienmuseum.at; 04, Karlsplatz; adult/child €5/free; 10am-6pm Tue-Sun Apr-Oct; U Karlsplatz)

## Akademie der Bildenden Künste
MUSEUM

4 MAP P102, F2

Founded in 1692, the Akademie der Bildenden Künste is an often-underrated art space. Its gallery concentrates on Flemish, Dutch and German painters, including important figures such as Hieronymus Bosch, Rembrandt, Van Dyck, Rubens, Titian, Francesco Guardi and Lucas Cranach the Elder. The supreme highlight is Bosch's macabre triptych of *The Last Judgment* altarpiece (1504–

08), depicting the banishment of Adam and Eve on the left panel, and the horror of Hell in the middle and right panels. Audio guides cost €2. (Academy of Fine Arts; www.akbild.ac.at; 01, Schillerplatz 3; adult/child €12/free; 10am-6pm Wed-Mon; D, 1, 2 Kärntner Ring/Oper, U Museumsquartier, Karlsplatz)

### Haydnhaus

MUSEUM

5 MAP P102, A5

Joseph Haydn (1732–1809) lived in Vienna during the heady times of Napoleon's occupation, and this exhibition at his last residence focuses on Vienna as well as London during the late 18th and early 19th centuries. Prominent in the classical period, Haydn is most celebrated for his 104 symphonies and 68 string quartets. The small garden here is modelled on Haydn's. Audio guides cost €4. (www.wienmuseum.at; 06, Haydngasse 19; adult/child €5/free, 1st Sun of month free; 10am-1pm & 2-6pm Tue-Sun; U Zieglergasse)

## Eating

### Vollpension

CAFE €

6 MAP P102, F3

This white-painted brick space with mismatched vintage furniture, tasselled lampshades and portraits on the walls is run by 15 *Omas* (grandmas) and *Opas* (grandpas) along with their families, with over 200 cakes in their collective repertoire. Breakfast, such as avocado and feta on pumpernickel bread, is served until 4pm; lunch dishes include a vegan

Karlskirche

BLUEJAYPHOTO/GETTY IMAGES ©

goulash with potato and tofu. Cash only. (www.vollpension.wien; 04, Schleifmühlgasse 16; dishes €5-10; 7.30am-10pm Mon-Sat, 8am-8pm Sun; ; U Karlsplatz)

## Said the Butcher to the Cow

BURGERS €€

7 MAP P102, F2

Not only does this wildly popular hangout have a brilliant name, it serves knock-out brioche-bun burgers (chicken teriyaki with wasabi mayo; black tiger prawns with bok choy; black bean patty with lotus root), chargrilled steaks, and house-speciality cheesecakes. Better yet, it moonlights as a **gin bar** with 30 gin varieties and seven different tonics. (01-535 69 69; www.butcher-cow.at; 01, Opernring 11; burgers €12-20.50, steaks €28.50-39; kitchen 2-10pm Tue & Wed, to 11pm Thu-Sat, bar 5pm-1am Tue & Wed, to 2am Thu-Sat; ; D, 1, 2, 71 Kärntner Ring/Oper, U Karlsplatz)

## Eis Greissler

ICE CREAM €

8 MAP P102, D2

The inevitable queue makes Eis Greissler easy to spot. Locals flock here – whatever the weather – for ice cream made from organic milk, yoghurt and cream from its own farm in Lower Austria. Vegans are well catered to with soy and oat milk varieties. All-natural flavours vary seasonally but might include goat's cheese, pumpkin-seed

## Meaningful Tourism

Vienna's tourism star continues to rise, hitting a record high of 16.5 million bed-nights in 2018, thanks in part to a raft of new flights. Crowd-pulling events, such as the centennial of the modernist era in 2018 and the 150th anniversary of the **Staatsoper** (p98) in 2019, have helped bolster these figures.

Despite this, travel here is increasingly meaningful thanks to a growing crop of social-tourism enterprises. These include the likes of **Magdas** (www.magdas-hotel.at), a boutique guesthouse run by refugees; **Vollpension** (p105), a retro-cool cafe where retirees bake cakes to bolster their pensions; and **Shades Tours** (p23), insightful city tours run by the city's homeless.

**Unhashtag Vienna** (www.unhashtag.vienna.info) is an initiative encouraging travellers to set their smartphones aside and stop seeing the city through the lens of social media, instead encouraging a deeper exploration of the city. A follow-up campaign, **Unrating Vienna** (www.unrating.wien.info), aims to counter online rating obsessions, asking visitors 'who decides what you like?'. Both campaigns aim to make travel in Vienna more rewarding.

oil, cinnamon, pear or marzipan. (www.eis-greissler.at; 06, Mariahilfer Strasse 33; 1/2/3/4/5 scoops €1.60/3/4.30/5.30/6; 11am-8pm; U Museumsquartier)

### Entler
AUSTRIAN €€

9 MAP P102, G5

While the setting beneath a vaulted ceiling is traditional, the cuisine here is cutting edge. Reinventions of Austrian classics include *Bergkässe* (hard cow's cheese) and black-truffle soup, pork medallions stuffed with apricots and smoked ham, roast hare strudel, and, for dessert, a walnut mousse sphere with hazelnut ice cream and candied hazelnut shards. (01-504 35 85; www.entler.at; 04, Schlüsselgasse 2; mains €14-28.50; 5-10pm Tue-Sat; ; 1, 62 Mayerhofgasse)

### Vegiezz
VEGAN €€

10 MAP P102, F1

In a bright, white space with sage-green chairs, pinewood floors and herbs growing in wall-mounted planter boxes, Vegiezz offers an all-vegan menu. It spans burgers, fries, quinotto (quinoa-based risotto) bowls, and desserts, such as avocado mousse with seasonal fruit, accompanied by homemade lemonade served in mason jar glasses. (01-890 00 32; www.vegiezz.at; 01, Opernring 6; dishes €8-14; 11am-10pm Mon-Fri, noon-11pm Sat, noon-10pm Sun; ; D, 1, 2, 71 Kärntner Ring, U Karlsplatz)

### Silberwirt
AUSTRIAN €€

11 MAP P102, D6

This atmospheric neo-*Beisl* offers traditional Viennese cuisine, mostly using organic and/or local produce. A meal might begin with Waldviertel sheep's cheese salad with walnuts and poppy seeds, followed by trout with parsley potatoes and almond butter, and *Palatschinken* (pancakes) with homemade apricot jam. A dedicated kids' menu appeals to little appetites. In summer, dine in the tree-shaded garden. (01-544 49 07; www.silberwirt.at; 05, Schlossgasse 21; mains €9-18; noon-midnight; ; U Pilgramgasse)

## Drinking

### Café Sperl
COFFEE

12 MAP P102, E3

With its gorgeous *Jugendstil* fittings, grand dimensions, cosy booths and unhurried air, 1880-opened Sperl is one of the finest coffee houses in Vienna. The must-try is *Sperl Torte*, an almond-and-chocolate-cream dream. Grab a slice and a newspaper, order a coffee (from some three dozen kinds) and join the people-watching patrons. A live pianist plays from 3.30pm to 5.30pm on Sundays. (www.cafesperl.at; 06, Gumpendorfer Strasse 11; 7am-10pm Mon-Sat, 10am-8pm Sun, closed Sun Jul & Aug; ; U Museumsquartier, Kettenbrückengasse)

## Vienna's LGBTIQ+ Scene

This neighbourhood is home to one of the city's liveliest LGBTIQ+ scenes. Popular venues include **Café Savoy** (Map p102, E3; www.savoy.at; 06, Linke Wienzeile 36; 10am-1am Mon-Thu, 10am-2am Fri, 9am-1am Sat, 9am-1am Sun; ; U Kettenbrückengasse), classy **Felixx** (Map p102, E2; www.felixx-bar.at; 06, Gumpendorfer Strasse 5; 10am-2am Sun-Thu, to 3am Fri & Sat; U Museumsquartier) and sociable **Mango Bar** (Map p102, E3; www.why-not.at; 06, Laimgrubengasse 3; 10pm-6am Fri & Sat; U Kettenbrückengasse).

The biggest annual LGBTIQ+ event is the **Regenbogen Parade** (Rainbow Parade; www.viennapride.at/regenbogenparade; mid-Jun). **Die Villa** (01-586 81 50; www.dievilla.at; 06, Linke Wienzeile 102; 5-8pm Mon, Wed & Fri; U Pilgramgasse) is Vienna's main point for LGBTIQ+ information.

### Café Schwarzenberg

CAFE

13 MAP P102, H2

One of the last remaining grand Viennese coffee houses on the Ringstrasse, this 1861 beauty has chandelier-lit vaulted ceilings, wood-panelled walls, marble tables, and studded leather seats. Secessionist architect and designer Josef Hoffmann was among its patrons and it still draws a local crowd for its coffee, international newspapers, flaky *Warmer Topfenstrudel* (warm cheese-curd strudel) and sublime *Sacher Torte*. (www.cafe-schwarzenberg.at; 01, Kärntner Ring 17; 7.30am-midnight Mon-Fri, 8.30am-midnight Sat & Sun; ; 2, 71 Schwarzenbergplatz)

### Barfly's Club

COCKTAIL BAR

14 MAP P102, B4

This sophisticated low-lit bar is famous for its extensive cocktail list and intimate ambience, which attracts a regular crowd of journalists and actors. It's decorated with photos of Ernest Hemingway, Fidel Castro, Che Guevara, Marilyn Monroe, plus the Rat Pack, whose music plays in the background. Drinks aren't cheap, but they're among the city's best. (www.barflys.at; 06, Esterházygasse 33; 6pm-2am Mon-Thu, to 4am Fri & Sat, 8pm-2am Sun; U Neubaugasse, Zieglergasse)

### Café Rüdigerhof

CAFE

15 MAP P102, C4

Rüdigerhof's facade is a glorious example of *Jugendstil* architecture, and the '50s furniture and fittings inside could be straight out of an *I Love Lucy* set. The atmosphere is homey and familiar, and the shaded wraparound garden huge. Hearty Austrian fare – huge schnitzels, spinach *Spätzle* (noodles), goat's cheese strudel – is way above average. On Saturday mornings it fills with Naschmarkt shoppers. (05, Hamburgerstrasse 20; 9am-2am; U Kettenbrückengasse, Pilgramgasse)

### Jakov's Weinkeller

WINE BAR

16 MAP P102, E3

Wine barrels double as tables outside Jakov's (a favourite with stallholders from the nearby Naschmarkt) with more seats inside at the wooden bar. Wines from Burgenland, Styria and Lower Austria's Weinviertel are specialities; there are also Hungarian reds and delicate Italian whites. Try them by the glass along with charcuterie and cheese platters, or pick up bottles to go. (04, Rechte Wienzeile 25-27; 11am-10pm Mon-Fri, to 11pm Sat; U Kettenbrückengasse)

### Café Jelinek

COFFEE

17 MAP P102, B4

With none of the polish or airs and graces of some other coffee houses, this shabbily grand cafe is Viennese through and through. The wood-burning stove, picture-plastered walls and faded velvet armchairs draw people from all walks of life with its cocoon-like warmth. Join locals lingering over freshly roasted coffee, cake and the daily newspapers. (www.steman.at; 06, Otto-Bauer-Gasse 5; 9am-10pm; ; U Zieglergasse)

### Club U

CLUB

18 MAP P102, G2

Club U occupies one of Otto Wagner's Stadtbahn Pavilions (p104) on Karlsplatz. It's a

Naschmarkt (p111)

PRESSDIGITAL/GETTY IMAGES ©

small, student-favourite bar-club with regular DJs and a wonderful outdoor seating area overlooking the pavilions and park. Happy hour runs from 9pm to 11pm. (www.club-u.at; 01, Künstlerhauspassage; 9pm-4am; ; U Karlsplatz)

# Entertainment

## Musikverein — CONCERT VENUE

19 MAP P102, H2

The opulent Musikverein holds the proud title of the concert hall with the best acoustics in Austria, and is embraced by the Vienna Philharmonic Orchestra. The lavish interior can be visited by 45-minute guided tour (in English; adult/child €8.50/5) at 1pm Tuesdays to Saturdays. Smaller-scale performances are held in the Brahms Saal. There are no student tickets. (01-505 81 90; www.musikverein.at; 01, Musikvereinsplatz 1; tickets €15-105, standing room €7-15; box office 9am-8pm Mon-Fri, to 1pm Sat Sep-Jun, 9am-noon Mon-Fri Jul & Aug; U Karlsplatz)

## Theater an der Wien — THEATRE

20 MAP P102, F3

The Theater an der Wien has hosted some monumental premiere performances, including Beethoven's *Fidelio*, Mozart's *The Magic Flute* and Johann Strauss II's *Die Fledermaus*. These days, besides staging musicals, dance and concerts, it's reestablished its reputation for high-quality opera. Student tickets go on sale 30 minutes before shows and standing-room tickets are available one hour prior to performances. (01-588 85-111; www.theater-wien.at; 06, Linke Wienzeile 6; tickets €5-165; box office 10am-6pm Mon-Sat, 2-6pm Sun; U Karlsplatz)

# Shopping

## Beer Lovers — DRINKS

21 MAP P102, D3

A wonderland of craft beers, this emporium stocks over 1000 labels from at least 125 breweries in more than 70 styles, with more being sourced every day. Tastings are offered regularly, and cold beers are available in the walk-in glass fridge and in refillable growlers. It also stocks craft ciders, small-batch liqueurs and boutique nonalcoholic drinks. (www.beer-lovers.at; 06, Gumpendorfer Strasse 35; 11am-8pm Mon-Fri, 10am-5pm Sat; U Kettenbrückengasse)

## Blühendes Konfekt — FOOD

22 MAP P102, A5

Violets, forest strawberries and cherry blossom, mint and oregano – Michael Diewald makes the most of what grows wild and in his garden to create confectionery that fizzes with seasonal flavour. Peek through to the workshop to see flowers and herbs being deftly transformed into one-of-a-kind bonbons and minibouquets that are edible works of art. Cash only. (0660 341 1985; www.bluehendes-konfekt.com; 06, Schmalzhofgasse 19; 10am-6.30pm Wed-Fri, by reservation Mon & Tue; U Zieglergasse, Westbahnhof)

## Vienna's Naschmarkt

Vienna's famous **market** (Map p102, F3; www.wien.gv.at; 06, Linke & Rechte Wienzeile; 6am-7.30pm Mon-Fri, to 5pm Sat; ; U Karlsplatz, Kettenbrückengasse) and eating strip began life as a farmers market in the 18th century, when the fruit market on Freyung was moved here. Interestingly, a law passed in 1793 said that fruit and vegetables arriving in town by cart had to be sold on Naschmarkt, while anything brought in by boat could be sold from the decks.

The fruits of the Orient poured in, the predecessors of the modern-day sausage stand were erected and sections were set aside for coal, wood and farming tools and machines. Officially, it became known as Naschmarkt ('munch market') in 1905, a few years after Otto Wagner bedded the Wien River down in its open-topped stone and concrete sarcophagus. This Otto Wagnerian horror was a blessing for Naschmarkt, because it created space to expand. A close shave came in 1965 when there were plans to tear it down – it was saved, and today the Naschmarkt is not only the place to shop for food but also to visit the **Flohmarkt** (Flea Market; Map p102, D4; 05, Linke Wienzeile; 6.30am-2pm Sat; U Kettenbrückengasse) each Saturday.

### Teuchtler Records

MUSIC

23 MAP P102, D3

Film fans will recognise Teuchtler Records from Richard Linklater's classic 1995 Vienna homage *Before Sunrise* – the promotional poster still hangs above the till. It jostles for pride of place among autographed headshots of jazz stars, punk-rock record posters and vintage gramophone players. This is a musical wonder covering everything from The Beatles to rare opera recordings. (01-586 21 33; www.schallplatten-ankauf-wien.com; Windmühlgasse 10; 1-6pm Mon & Fri, 10am-1pm Sat; U Neubaugasse)

### Gabarage Upcycling Design

DESIGN

24 MAP P102, F4

Recycled design, ecology and social responsibility underpin the quirky designs at Gabarage. Old bowling pins become vases, rubbish bins get a new life as tables and chairs, advertising tarpaulins morph into bags, and traffic lights are transformed into funky lights. (www.gabarage.at; 04, Schleifmühlgasse 6; 10am-6pm Mon-Thu, 7pm Fri, 11am-5pm Sat; U Taubstummengasse)

BAROCK

Explore

# Schloss Belvedere to the Canal

***The crowning glory of this art-rammed neighbourhood is Schloss Belvedere and its gardens. Spread out across the neighbourhood, other crowd-pullers include the kaleidoscopic KunstHausWien, as well as museums homing in on everything from military history to art fakes. Some cracking cafes and restaurants make breaks between sightseeing all the more pleasurable.***

## The Short List

- ***Schloss Belvedere & Gardens (p114)*** *Drawing breath as you ramble through lavishly frescoed apartments, sculpture-strewn gardens and a gallery home to the ultimate embrace: Klimt's The Kiss.*
- ***Heeresgeschichtliches Museum (p124)*** *Having shivers sent down your spine as you venture through Vienna's war-torn history.*
- ***KunstHausWien (p125)*** *Being dazzled by Hundertwasser's wonky floors, madcap mosaics and hallucinatory colours.*
- ***Museum für Angewandte Kunst (p124)*** *Rewinding a century to the dawn of a modernist age.*
- ***Belvedere 21 (p119)*** *Zooming in on contemporary art with an Austrian slant at this modernist gallery.*

## Getting There & Around

U Taubstummengasse and Südtiroler Platz stations, both on the U1 line, are close to Schloss Belvedere.

Trams trump the U-Bahn for access to some parts of the 3rd district. Tram 2 trundles around the Ring (for MAK, Stadtpark), tram 1 to Radetzkyplatz (for the Hundertwasser sights).

**Schloss Belvedere to the Canal Map on p122**

**Museum für Angewandte Kunst (p124)** VVOE/SHUTTERSTOCK ©

Top Experience

# Stroll in Schloss Belvedere & Gardens

*A masterpiece of total art, Belvedere is one of the world's finest baroque palaces. Designed by Johann Lukas von Hildebrandt (1668–1745), it was built as a summer residence for the brilliant military strategist Prince Eugene of Savoy, conqueror of the Turks in 1718. Eugene had grown up around the court of Louis XIV and it shows – this is a chateau to rival Versailles.*

MAP P122, C6

www.belvedere.at

adult/child Oberes Belvedere €16/free, Unteres Belvedere €14/free

9am-6pm Sat-Thu, to 9pm Fri

D, 71 Schwarzenbergplatz

U Taubstummengasse, Südtiroler Platz

## Oberes Belvedere

Rising splendidly above the gardens and commanding sweeping views of Vienna's skyline, the **Oberes Belvedere** (Upper Belvedere; 03, Prinz-Eugen-Strasse 27) is one of Vienna's unmissable sights. Built between 1717 and 1723, its peerless art collection, showcased in rooms replete with marble, frescoes and stucco, attests to the unfathomable wealth and cultured tastes of the Habsburg Empire.

The **Sala Terrena** is a grand prelude to the ground floor, with four colossal Atlas pillars supporting the weight of its delicately stuccoed vault. Spread across four beautifully frescoed rooms, **Medieval Art** leads you through the artistic development of the age, with an exceptional portfolio of Gothic sculpture and altarpieces, many from Austrian abbeys and monasteries. Top billing goes to the Master of Grosslobming's sculptural group, whose fluid, expressive works embodied the figurative ideal; among them is the faceless *St George with Dragon* (1395), with a rather tame-looking dragon at St George's feet. Other heavenly treasures include Joachim's polyptych *Albrechtsaltar* (1435), one of the foremost examples of Gothic realism, and the *Znaim Altar* (1445), a gilded glorification of faith showing the Passion of Christ.

**Modern Art & Interwar Period** is particularly strong on Austrian expressionism. Attention-grabbers here include Oskar Kokoschka's richly animated portrait of art-nouveau painter *Carl Moll* (1913). Egon Schiele is represented by works both haunting and beguiling, such as *Death and the Maiden* (1915) and his portrait of six-year-old *Herbert Rainer* (1910). Other standouts include Oskar Laske's staggeringly detailed *Ship of Fools* (1923) and Max Oppenheimer's musical

### ★ Top Tips

- Order tickets online to save time and money.
- Visit the website for details on guided tours and upcoming exhibitions.
- Dodge the crowds by arriving just before the palace opens – queues are at their worst at peak summer times.

### Take a Break

Take a five-minute stroll to **15 Süsse Minuten** (☎0664 4729 060; www.15suesseminuten.at; 04, Favoritenstrasse 45; breakfast €5-13, mains €10-18; 8am-6pm; U Hauptbahnhof) for cakes, good strong coffee or a light lunch.

masterpiece *The Philharmonic* (1935), with a baton-swinging Gustav Mahler.

The 1st-floor **Vienna 1880–1914** collection is a holy grail for Klimt fans, with an entire room devoted to erotic golden wonders such as *Judith* (1901), *Salome* (1909), *Adam and Eve* (1917) and *The Kiss* (1908). Works by German symbolist painter Max Klinger (1857–1920), as well as portraits by Secessionist Koloman Moser and Norwegian expressionist Edvard Munch, also feature.

The centrepiece is the **Marmorsaal**, a chandelier-lit marble, stucco and *trompe l'oeil* confection, crowned by Carlo Innocenzo Carlone's ceiling fresco (1721–23) celebrating the glorification of Prince Eugene. **Baroque & Early-19th-Century Art** pays tribute to Austrian masters of the age, endowed with highlights such as Johann Michael Rottmayr's lucid *Susanna and the Elders* (1692) and Paul Troger's chiaroscuro *Christ on the Mount of Olives* (1750).

**Neoclassicism, Romanticism & Biedermeier Art** has outstanding works such as Georg Waldmüller's *Corpus Christi Morning* (1857), a joyous snapshot of impish lads and flower girls bathed in honeyed light. Representative of the neoclassical period are clearer, more emotionally restrained pieces such as Jacques-Louis David's gallant *Napoleon on Great St Bernard Pass* (1801) and François Gérard's portrait *Count Moritz Christian Fries and Family* (1804). The romantic period is headlined by the wistful, brooding landscapes and seascapes of 19th-century German painter Caspar David Friedrich.

## Schloss Belvedere & Gardens

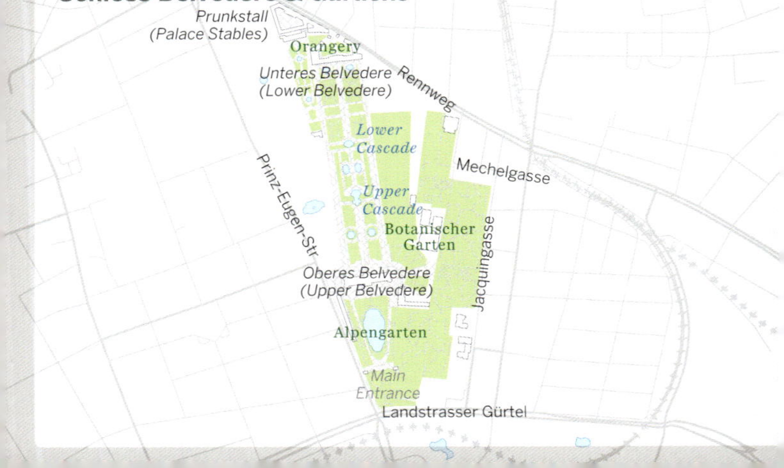

## Adele Bloch-Bauer

The Nazis seized the property of the wealthy Jewish Bloch-Bauer family following the 1938 *Anschluss* (annexation). Among their substantial collection were five Klimt originals, including the *Portrait of Adele Bloch-Bauer I* (1907). The stolen paintings hung in the Oberes Belvedere until 2006, when a US Supreme Court ruled the Austrian government must return the paintings to their rightful owner, Adele Bloch-Bauer's niece and heir Maria Altmann. The portrait alone fetched US$135 million at auction, at the time the highest price paid for a painting, and today hangs in the New York Neue Galerie.

French masters share the limelight with their Austrian and German contemporaries in **Realism & Impressionism**, where you'll feel the artistic pull of Renoir's softly evocative *Woman after the Bath* (1876), Monet's sun-dappled *Garden at Giverny* (1902) and Van Gogh's *Plain at Auvers* (1890), where wheat fields ripple under a billowing sky. Lovis Corinth's tranquil *Woman Reading Near a Goldfish Tank* (1911) and Max Liebermann's *Hunter in the Dunes* (1913) epitomise the German impressionist style.

## Gardens

Belvedere means 'beautiful view' and the reason for this name becomes apparent in the baroque garden linking the upper and lower palaces, which was laid out around 1700 in classical French style by Dominique Girard, a pupil of André le Nôtre of Versailles fame. Set along a central axis, the gently sloping garden commands a broad view of Vienna's skyline, with Stephansdom and the Hofburg punctuating the horizon.

The three-tiered garden is lined by clipped box hedges and flanked by ornamental parterres. As you stroll to the **Lower Cascade**, with its frolicking water nymphs, look out for Greco-Roman statues of the eight muses and cherubic putti embodying the 12 months of the year. Mythical beasts squirt water across the **Upper Cascade**, which spills down five steps into the basin below. Guarding the approach to the Oberes Belvedere are winged sphinxes, symbols of power and wisdom, which look as though they are about to take flight any minute.

South of the Oberes Belvedere is the **Alpengarten** (www.bundesgaerten.at; adult/child €3.50/2.50; 10am-6pm late Mar-early Aug; D, O Quartier Belvedere, U Hauptbahnhof), a Japanese-style garden nurturing alpine species, at its fragrant best from spring to summer, when clematis, rhododendrons, roses and peonies are in bloom. North from here is the larger **Botanischer Garten** (www.botanik.univie.ac.at; 03, Mechelgasse/

Praetoriusgasse; admission free; 10am-6pm; 0, 1, 71 Rennweg), belonging to the Vienna University, with tropical glasshouses and 11,500 botanical species, including Chinese dwarf bamboo and Japanese plum yews.

## Unteres Belvedere

Built between 1712 and 1716, **Unteres Belvedere** (Lower Belvedere; 03, Rennweg 6) is a baroque feast of state apartments and ceremonial rooms. Most lavish of all is the red marble **Marmorsaal**, an ode to Prince Eugene's military victories, with stucco trophies, medallions and Martino Altomonte's ceiling fresco showing the glorification of the prince and Apollo surrounded by muses. At eye level are sculptures taken from Georg Raphael Donner's mid-18th-century fountain on Neuer Markt. Snake-bearing Providentia (Prudence) rises above four putti grappling with fish, each of which symbolises a tributary of the Danube (Donau).

In the **Groteskensaal**, foliage intertwines with fruit, birds and mythological beasts in the fanciful grotesque style that was all the rage in baroque times. This leads through to the **Marmorgalerie**, a vision of frilly white stucco and marble, encrusted with cherubs and war trophies. The niches originally displayed three classical statues from Herculaneum (now in Dresden), which inspired baroque sculptor Domenico Parodi to create the neoclassical statues you see today. Maria Theresia put her stamp on the palace in the adjacent

Medieval paintings, Schloss Belvedere

**Goldkabinett**, a mirrored cabinet dripping in gold.

Temporary exhibitions are held in the **Orangery**, with a walkway gazing grandly over Prince Eugene's private garden. Attached to the Orangery is the **Prunkstall**, the former royal stables, where you can now trot through a 150-piece collection of Austrian medieval art, including religious scenes, altarpieces, sculpture and Gothic triptychs.

## Belvedere 21

The modernist, glass-and-steel **Austria Pavilion**, designed by Karl Schwanzer for Expo 58 in Brussels, was reborn as **Belvedere 21** (www.belvedere21.at; 03, Arsenalstrasse 1; adult/under 18yr €8/free; 11am-6pm Wed-Sun, to 9pm Fri; 0, 1, 18 Fasangasse, U Hauptbahnhof) in 2011, with exhibitions devoted to 20th- and 21st-century art, predominantly with an Austrian focus. Adolf Krischanitz left his clean aesthetic imprint on the open-plan gallery, which sits just south of the Oberes Belvedere in the **Schweizergarten**.

The gallery's dynamic approach embraces an artist-in-residence scheme and a changing rota of contemporary exhibitions. On permanent display is a peerless collection of sculptures by Viennese artist **Fritz Wotruba** (1907–75), many of which deconstruct the human form into a series of abstract, geometric shapes that have more than an element of cubism about them.

## Combined Tickets

Ordering printable tickets online saves time, but they can't be exchanged or refunded. Several money-saving combined ticket options are available, including one covering the Upper Belvedere and Lower Belvedere (adult/under 19 years €22/free), and one additionally covering Belvedere 21 (adult/under 19 years €25/free). Combined tickets are valid for two weeks after the first visit.

## Guided Tours

Audio guides can be hired for €5 at the Upper Belvedere and €4 at the Lower Belvedere, and are available in German, English, French, Italian, Spanish, Japanese and Russian; you'll need to leave ID as a form of deposit. One-hour themed tours shedding light on a specific period or artist cost €4 and are in German. Times and themes vary (see the online calendar), but generally there are tours at 3pm and/or 4pm on weekends, plus 10.30am on Sundays.

LUKAS SCHALLER/BELVEDERE, VIENNA ©

## Walking Tour

# Green Escape

*Get a breath of fresh air on this stroll, which starts at a farmers market, stops off for coffee and passes some of Vienna's most adventurous architecture before bringing you down to the parkland-lined Danube Canal (Donaukanal). More parks along this green route include the Stadtpark (city park) and beautiful botanic gardens.*

### Walk Facts

**Start** Rochusmarkt (U Rochusgasse)

**End** Botanischer Garten (tram 0, 1, 71 Rennweg)

**Length** 4.6km; 90 minutes to four hours

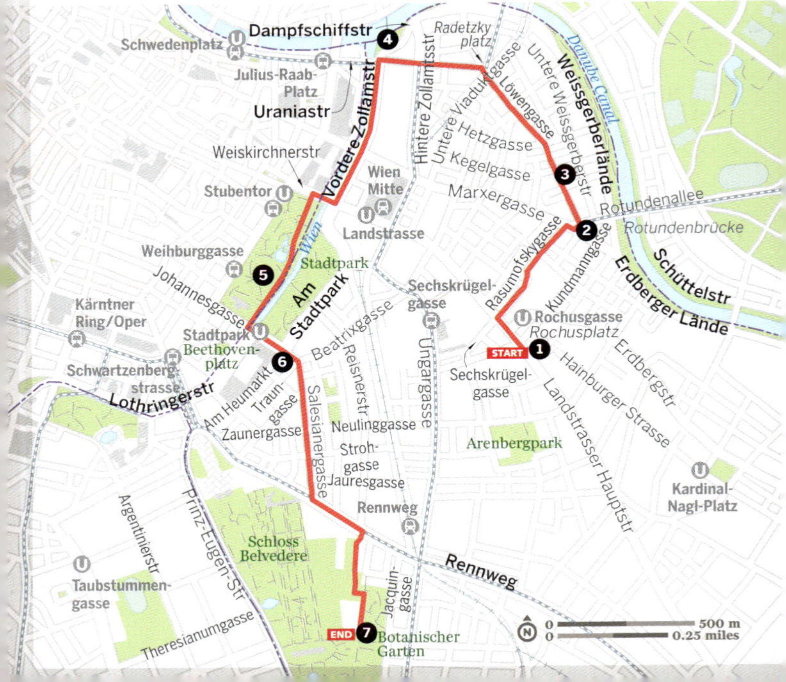

## ❶ Market Shop

The stalls are piled high with olives, flowers, farm-fresh meat and cheese at the **Rochusmarkt** (03, Landstrasser Hauptstrasse; 6am-7.30pm Mon-Fri, to 5pm Sat). There are a handful of cafes, takeaway joints and bakeries on the square.

## ❷ Coffee Stop

A withered beauty of a coffee house, **Café Zartl** (03, Rasumofskygasse 7; 7am-10pm; ; 1 Rasumofskygasse) pings you back to when it opened in 1883, with its striped banquettes, cocoon-like warmth and delightfully flaky strudel.

## ❸ Radical Architecture

Apartment block **Hundert-wasserhaus** (03, cnr Löwengasse & Kegelgasse) bears all the wackily creative hallmarks of Vienna's radical architect Hundertwasser with its curvy lines, crayon-bright colours and mosaics. Across the road, cafe- and shop-filled Kalke Village is also the handiwork of Hundertwasser, created from an old Michelin factory. In typical Hundertwasser fashion, it has colourful ceramics and a distinct absence of straight lines.

## ❹ Beach Bar

You'd swear you're by the sea at hopping canal-side **Strandbar Herrmann** (p128), with beach chairs, sand, DJ beats and Viennese livin' it up on summer evenings. Cocktails are two for the price of one during happy hour (6pm to 7pm). It's located on Herrmannpark, named after picture-postcard inventor Emanuel Herrmann (1839–1902).

## ❺ Park Life

Opened in 1862, the **Stadtpark** (City Park; admission free) is a tranquil pocket of greenery, with winding paths and willow tree-rimmed duck ponds. It's great for strolling or relaxing in the sun and is a favourite lunchtime escape for Innere Stadt workers. The park spans the Wien River, which empties into the Danube Canal.

## ❻ Hidden Cafe

Look for the house number, not the name, as there's no sign at **Café am Heumarkt** (03, Am Heumarkt 15; 9am-11pm Mon-Fri), an old-school charmer of a coffee house. Inside, it's a 1950s time-warp – all shiny parquet, leather banquettes and marble tables.

## ❼ Botanic Gardens

The **Botanischer Garten** (p117), belonging to the Vienna University, have tropical glasshouses and 11,500 species from six continents, including botanical wonders like Chinese dwarf bamboo, gingko biloba, tulip trees and Japanese plum yews.

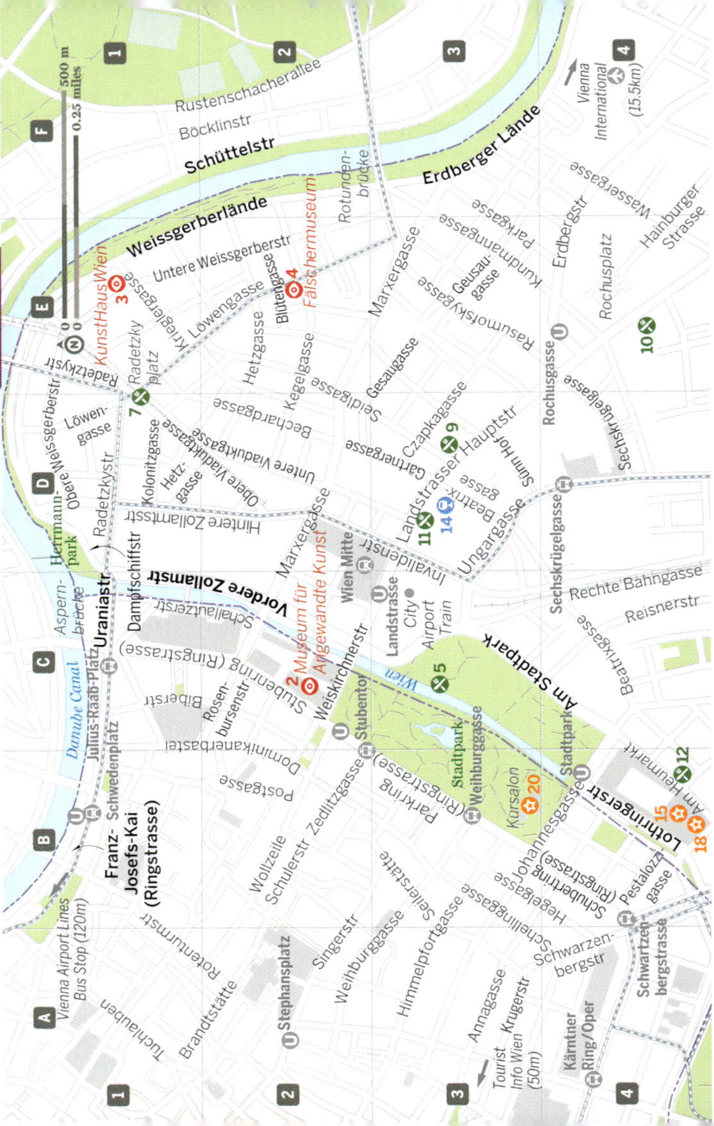
A
B
C
D
E
F
1
2
3
4
500 m
0.25 miles
Rustenschacherallee
Böcklinstr
Schüttelstr
Weissgerberlände
Erdberger Lände
Rotunden-brücke
Untere Weissgerberstr
Radetzkystr
Obere Weissgerberstr
Löwen-gasse
Herrmann-park
Aspern-brücke
Uraniastr
Radetzkystr
Dampfschiffstr
Kriegleregasse
Löwengasse
Blütengasse
3 KunstHausWien
4 Fälschermuseum
Radetzky platz
7
Kolonitzgasse
Hetzgasse
Kegelgasse
Hetz-gasse
Bechardgasse
Untere Viaduktgasse
Obere Viaduktgasse
Hintere Zollamtsstr
Vordere Zollamstr
Marxergasse
Seidlgasse
Gesaugasse
Gärtnergasse
Czapkagasse
9
Landstrasser Hauptstr
11
14
Beatrix-gasse
Sünn Hof
Ungargasse
Invalidenstr
Wien Mitte
Landstrasse
City Airport Train
Rasumofskygasse
Geusau-gasse
Kundmanngasse
Parkgasse
Wassergasse
Erdbergstr
Rochusgasse
Rochusplatz
Sechskrügelgasse
Hainburger Strasse
Vienna International (15.5km)
10
Rechte Bahngasse
Reisnerstr
Beatrixgasse
Sechskrügelgasse
Am Stadtpark
Danube Canal
Julius-Raab-Platz
Schwedenplatz
Franz-Josefs-Kai (Ringstrasse)
Vienna Airport Lines Bus Stop (120m)
Schallautzerstr
Stubenring (Ringstrasse)
2 Museum für Angewandte Kunst
Biberstr
Rosen-bursenstr
Weiskirchnerstr
Stubentor
Wien
5
Dominikanerbastei
Postgasse
Zedlitzgasse
Parkring (Ringstrasse)
Stadtpark
Weihburggasse
Kursalon
20
Stadtpark
Johannesgasse
Lothringerstr
Am Heumarkt
12
15
18
Pestalozzi-gasse
Schubertring (Ringstrasse)
Hegelgasse
Schellinggasse
Seilerstätte
Himmelpfortgasse
Weihburggasse
Singerstr
Wollzeile
Schulerstr
Stephansplatz
Rotenturmstr
Brandstätte
Tuchlauben
Annagasse
Krugerstr
Tourist Info Wien (50m)
Schwarzen-bergstr
Schwartzen-bergstrasse
Kärntner Ring/Oper

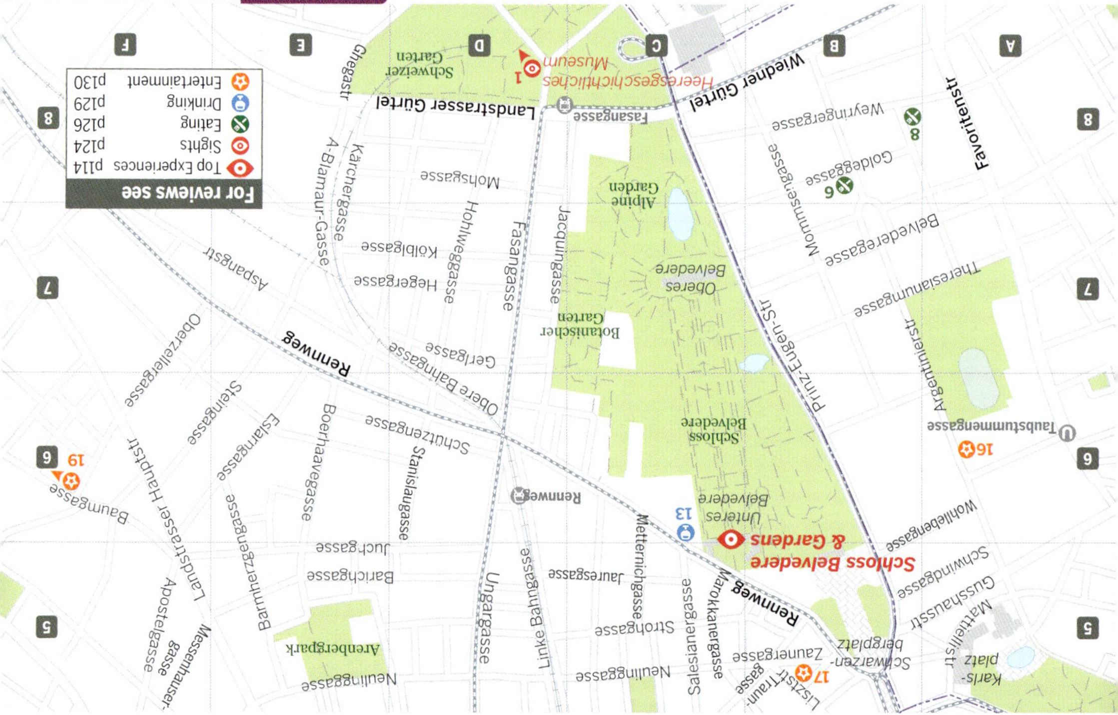
For reviews see
Top Experiences p114
Sights p124
Eating p126
Drinking p129
Entertainment p130
Schloss Belvedere & Gardens
Heeresgeschichtliches Museum
Schloss Belvedere
Unteres Belvedere
Oberes Belvedere
Botanischer Garten
Alpine Garden
Schweizer Garten
Arenbergpark
Rennweg
Landstrasser Gürtel
Wiedner Gürtel
Prinz-Eugen-Str
Landstrasser Hauptstr
Favoritenstr
Argentinierstr
Taubstummengasse
Karlsplatz
Schwarzenbergplatz
Fasangasse
Jacquingasse
Ungargasse
Linke Bahngasse
Obere Bahngasse
Aspangstr
Oberzellergasse
Steingasse
Eslarngasse
Barmherzgengasse
Boerhaavegasse
Schützengasse
Stanislausgasse
Juchgasse
Barichgasse
Neulinggasse
Jauresgasse
Strohgasse
Salesianergasse
Metternichgasse
Marokkanergasse
Zaunergasse
Lisztstr
Traungasse
Mommsengasse
Goldeggasse
Weyringergasse
Belvederegasse
Theresianumgasse
Wohllebengasse
Schwindgasse
Gusshausstr
Mattiellistr
Hegergasse
Kölblgasse
Hohlweggasse
Mohsgasse
Gerlgasse
Kärchergasse
A-Blamaur-Gasse
Ghegastr
Baumgasse
Apostelgasse
Messenhausergasse
1
6
8
13
16
17
19
A
B
C
D
E
F
5
6
7
8

# Sights

## Heeresgeschichtliches Museum

MUSEUM

1 MAP P122, D8

This superb museum is housed in the Arsenal, a large neo-Byzantine barracks and munitions depot. Spread over two floors, it works its way from the Thirty Years' War (1618–48) to WWII, taking in the Hungarian Uprising and the Austro-Prussian War (ending in 1866), the Napoleonic and Turkish Wars, and WWI. Highlights on the 1st floor include the Great Seal of Mustafa Pasha, which fell to Prince Eugene of Savoy in the Battle of Zenta in 1697. (Museum of Military History; www.hgm.at; 03, Arsenal; adult/under 19yr €7/free, 1st Sun of month free; 9am-5pm; U Südtiroler Platz)

## Museum für Angewandte Kunst

MUSEUM

2 MAP P122, C2

MAK is devoted to craftsmanship and art forms in everyday life. Each exhibition room showcases a different style, including Renaissance, baroque, orientalism and the distinctive metalwork of the Wiener Werkstätte. Contemporary artists were invited to present the rooms in ways they felt were appropriate, resulting in eye-catching and unique displays. The 20th-century design and architecture room is fascinating, and Frank Gehry's cardboard chair is a gem. (Museum of Applied Arts; www.mak.at; 01, Stubenring 5; adult/under 19yr €12/free, 6-10pm Tue €5, tours €3.50; 10am-6pm Wed-Sun, to 10pm Tue, English tours noon Sun; 2 Stubentor, U Stubentor)

Heeresgeschichtliches Museum

YURI TURKOV/SHUTTERSTOCK ©

## 'The End of the Line': Zentralfriedhof

When a Wiener says, *'Er hat den 71er genommen'* ('He took the No 71'), they are, metaphorically speaking, referring to the end of the line: **Zentralfriedhof** (www.friedhoefewien.at; 11, Simmeringer Hauptstrasse 232-244; 7am-8pm, shorter hours in winter; 6, 71 Zentralfriedhof). The cemetery's mammoth scale (2.4 sq km, more than three million resting residents) has made its tram line a euphemism for death. One of Europe's biggest cemeteries, this is where rich and poor, Buddhists and Jews, Catholics and Protestants lie side by side in eternal slumber under ash and maple trees. With leafy avenues and overgrown monuments, it is a remarkably calming place to wander.

The information centre and map of the cemetery are at Gate Two. Just beyond are the all-star **Ehrengräber** (Tombs of Honour). Besides the clump of big-name composers such as Beethoven, Brahms, Johann Strauss Father and Son, and Schubert, lie Austrian luminaries including artist Hans Makart, sculptor Fritz Wotruba, architect Adolf Loos and 1980s pop icon Falco. Mozart may have a monument here, but he is buried in an unmarked grave in the **St Marxer Friedhof** (Cemetery of St Marx; www.friedhoefewien.at; 03, Leberstrasse 6-8; 6.30am-8pm Apr-Sep, to 6.30pm Oct-Mar; U Zippererstrasse).

### KunstHausWien MUSEUM

3 MAP P122, E1

The KunstHausWien, with its bulging ceramics, wonky surfaces, checkerboard facade, Technicolor mosaic tilework and rooftop sprouting plants and trees, bears the inimitable hallmark of eccentric Viennese artist and ecowarrior Friedensreich Hundertwasser (1928–2000), who famously called the straight line 'godless'. It is an ode to his playful, boldly creative work, as well as to his green politics. (Art House Vienna; www.kunsthauswien.com; 03, Untere Weissgerberstrasse 13; adult/child €12/5; 10am-6pm; 0, 1 Radetzkyplatz)

### Fälschermuseum MUSEUM

4 MAP P122, E2

Wow, a museum with Schiele, Raphael, Rembrandt and Marc Chagall paintings that nobody knows about? Well, that's because they are all fakes, though spotting the difference is a near impossibility. This tiny, privately run museum opens a fascinating window on the world of art forgeries. As well as background on the who, how, when and what, the museum recounts stories about master forgers who briefly managed to pull the wool over the experts' eyes. (Museum of Art Fakes; www.faelschermuseum.com; 03, Löwengasse 28; adult/child €6/3.20; 10am-5pm Tue-Sun; 1 Hetzgasse)

## Gustav Klimt in Vienna

The works of Gustav Klimt (1862–1918) – the shining star of Austria's *Jugendstil* age – are as resonant and alluring today as they were when he sent ripples of scandal through the rigid artistic establishment in *fin de siècle* Vienna with his exotic, erotic style.

### Judith (1901; Upper Belvedere)

One of Klimt's seminal art works, this is an entrancing evocation of the Old Testament heroine Judith, a rich widow who charms and decapitates Holofernes (look for his severed head in the right-hand corner of the canvas). The use of gold-leaf and mosaic-like detail is typical of Klimt's golden period, which was inspired by the Byzantine imagery he saw on his travels to Venice.

### The Kiss (1908; Upper Belvedere)

A couple draped in elaborate robes are shown entwined in an embrace in a flowered meadow. With a sinuous waterfall of gold-leaf and elaborate patterning set against a stardust backdrop, the couple appear to transgress the canvas with their dreamlike, rapturous state.

### Adam & Eve (1918; Upper Belvedere)

Klimt was working on this biblical wonder when he suddenly died of a stroke on 6 February 1918. Adam is less prominent in the background, while in the foreground stands Eve, with a cascade of golden hair and anemones scattered at her feet.

# Eating

### Steirereck im Stadtpark GASTRONOMY **€€€**

5 MAP P122, C3

Heinz Reitbauer is at the culinary helm of this two-starred Michelin restaurant, beautifully lodged in a 20th-century former dairy building in the leafy Stadtpark. His tasting menus are an exuberant feast, fizzing with natural, integral flavours that speak of a chef with exacting standards. Wine pairing is an additional €79/89 (six/seven courses). (01-713 31 68; http://steirereck.at; 03, Am Heumarkt 2a; mains €38-58, 6-/7-course menus €149/165; 11.30am-2.30pm & 6.30pm-midnight Mon-Fri; U Stadtpark)

### Café Goldegg CAFE **€**

6 MAP P122, B8

Goldegg is a coffee house in the classic Viennese mould, with its green-velvet booths, wood panelling, billiard tables and art nouveau sheen – but with a twist. Staff are refreshingly attentive, and alongside menu stalwarts, such as goulash, you'll find lighter dishes like toasted paninis with home-made basil pesto and Ayurvedic vegetable curries. (www.cafegoldegg.at; 04, Argentinierstrasse 49; snacks €3.50-6, mains €10-14; 8am-8pm Mon-Fri, from 9am Sat, 9am-7pm Sun; ; U Südtiroler Platz)

## Meierei im Stadtpark

AUSTRIAN **€€**

In the green surrounds of Stadtpark (see **5** Map p122, C3), the Meierei is most famous for its goulash served with lemon, capers and creamy dumplings, and its selection of 120 types of cheese. Served until noon, the bountiful breakfast features gastronomic showstoppers, such as poached duck egg with forest mushrooms and pumpkin, and corn waffles with warm tomato salad and sheep's cheese. (01-713 31 68; www.steirereck.at; 03, Am Heumarkt 2a; mains €19-22, set breakfasts €21-25; 8am-11pm Mon-Fri, 9am-7pm Sat & Sun; ; U Stadtpark)

## Garage 01

INTERNATIONAL **€**

**7** MAP P122, D1

One of the hippest kids on the block, this bar-restaurant under the railway viaduct arches goes for the stylishly distressed look, with raw brickwork, peeling plaster and bentwood chairs. Come for cocktails, the occasional gig and a bite to eat – there's everything from tapas to mains like wild garlic, asparagus and pea risotto, and short ribs with wasabi and king oyster mushrooms. (01-308 45 03; www.garage01.at; 03, Viaduktbogen 5; lunch €8.90-9.80, mains €11-19; noon-midnight Tue & Wed, to 2am Thu-Sat; O, 1 Radetzkyplatz)

## Das Lokal in Hof

INTERNATIONAL **€**

**8** MAP P122, B8

Snuggled away in the courtyard of an old dairy is this cracking cafe-restaurant, with a stripped-back interior and an open kitchen. The owners run the place with love and an imaginative eye, serving food that is honest, generous and delicious – be it asparagus gnocchi with rocket, Parmesan and cashews, or salmon trout with silver beets and caper popcorn. (01-971 91 41; https://daslokal.at; 04, Viktorgasse 22; mains €11.90-17.90, lunch special €7.60-8.60; 11am-11pm Mon-Fri; U Hauptbahnhof)

## Heunisch & Erben

AUSTRIAN **€€**

**9** MAP P122, D3

This contemporary wine bar and restaurant has carved out a reputation for itself in gastro circles. It's a minimalist, high-ceilinged space, with tall arched windows, bare wood tables and an assemblage of wine crates dangling from the ceiling. The Mediterranean meets Austria in dishes like aubergine with yellow pepper, linseed and stracchino cheese, and tender pork cheeks with root-vegetable mash. (01-286 85 63; www.heunisch.at; 03, Landstrasser Hauptstrasse 17; mains €22-29, 4-/5-course menu €52-62; 3pm-1am Tue-Sat; U Landstrasse)

### Lingenhel

EUROPEAN €€

10 MAP P122, E4

Lingenhel is an ultraslick deli-shop-bar-restaurant, lodged in a 200-year-old house. Salamis, wines and own-dairy cheeses tempt in the shop, while the pared-back, white-washed restaurant has season-inflected modern European food. As simple as trout with peas, turnip and orange, this is food that tastes profoundly of what it ought to. (01-710 15 66; www.lingenhel.com; 03, Landstrasser Hauptstrasse 74; lunch €10-13, mains €17-26; 8am-10pm Mon-Sat; U Rochusgasse)

### Joseph Brot

BISTRO €€

11 MAP P122, D3

Purveyors of Vienna's finest bread, Joseph Brot's bakery, bistro and patisserie is a winner. Besides wonderfully fresh loaves – organic olive-tomato ciabatta and rye-honey-lavender, for instance – it does wholesome breakfasts, speciality teas, healthy smoothies and yummy pastries. Season-driven specials such as sourdough *Spätzle* (noodles) with mountain cheese, lemon shallots and hispi cabbage star on the lunch menu in the stripped-back bistro. (www.joseph.co.at; 03, Landstrasser Hauptstrasse 4; breakfast €6.90-14.80, lunch mains €10-16.50; bakery 7.30am-9pm Mon-Fri, 8am-6pm Sat & Sun, bistro 8am-9pm Mon-Fri, to 6pm Sat & Sun; U Wien Mitte)

### Gmoakeller

AUSTRIAN €€

12 MAP P122, B4

Sizzling and stirring since 1858, this atmospheric cellar is as traditional as it gets, with parquet

## Summer Haunts: Schanigärten

When the weather warms up, Viennese life spills outdoors to the *Schanigärten* (pavement cafe). Unlike *Gastgärten* (beer gardens), *Schanigärten* set up on public property such as pavements and sometimes parking areas and squares according to inexpensive permits issued by authorities, which are valid from 1 March to 15 November. Actual opening dates depend on the weather each season.

Beach bars pop up along the waterfront in summer and include **Tel Aviv Beach** (https://neni.at/restaurants/tel-aviv-beach-bar; 02, Obere Donaustrasse 65; noon-midnight Apr-Oct; U Schottenring) and **Strandbar Herrmann** (www.strandbarherrmann.at; 03, Herrmannpark; 10am-2am Apr-early Oct; ; O Hintere Zollamstrasse, U Schwedenplatz). They're a great alternative for Viennese who don't join their fellow citizens decamping from the city to the Austrian lakes during the July/August *Sommerpause* (summer break), when many of the city's restaurants, bars and smaller shops shut down.

BOGGY22/GETTY IMAGES ©

Architect Friedensreich Hundertwasser's KunstHausWien (p125)

floors, brick vaults and warm wood panelling. The classic grub – *Zwiebelrostbraten* (onion-topped roast beef) or Carinthian *Kas'nudeln* (cheese noodles) – goes nicely with tangy Austrian wines. Tables spill out onto the pavement in summer. (☎01-712 53 10; www.gmoakeller.at; 03, Am Heumarkt 25; lunch €8.20, mains €10-18; ⏰11am-midnight Mon-Sat; U Stadtpark)

## Drinking

### Salm Bräu

MICROBREWERY

13 MAP P122, C6

Salm Bräu brews its own *Helles*, *Pils* (pilsner), *Märzen* (red-coloured beer with a strong malt taste), *G'mischt* (half *Helles* and half *Dunkel* – dark) and *Weizen* (full-bodied wheat beer, slightly sweet in taste). It is smack next to Schloss Belvedere and hugely popular. (www.salmbraeu.com; 03, Rennweg 8; ⏰11am-midnight; 🚊71 Unteres Belvedere, U Karlsplatz)

### Laniato: Wiener Wollcafe

CAFE

14 MAP P122, D3

Locals are spinning a yarn (pardon the pun) about this relaxed knitting cafe. Come here to sip a coffee, nibble on a brownie and watch the needles flying as you browse colourful yarns and wooly creations. (www.laniato.com; 03, Beatrixgasse 4; ⏰10am-1pm & 2-6pm Mon-Fri, 9.30am-5pm Sat; U Landstrasse)

# Entertainment

## Konzerthaus

CONCERT VENUE

15 MAP P122, B4

The Konzerthaus is a major venue in classical-music circles, but throughout the year ethnic music, rock, pop or jazz can also be heard in its hallowed halls. Up to three simultaneous performances, in the Grosser Saal, the Mozart Saal and the Schubert Saal, can be staged; this massive complex also features another four concert halls. (01-242 002; www.konzerthaus.at; 03, Lothringerstrasse 20; box office 9am-7.45pm Mon-Fri, 10am-2pm Sat, plus 45min before performance; D Gusshausstrasse, U Stadtpark)

## Radiokulturhaus

CONCERT VENUE

16 MAP P122, A6

The line-up here swings from classical concerts to jazz quartets and cabaret. Housed in several performance venues including the Grosser Sendesaal (home to the Vienna Radio Symphony Orchestra and the Klangtheater), this is one of Vienna's cultural hotspots. (01-501 703 77; http://radiokulturhaus.orf.at; 04, Argentinierstrasse 30a; tickets €19; box office 4-7pm Mon-Fri; D Plösslgasse, U Taubstummengasse)

## Arnold Schönberg Center

CLASSICAL MUSIC

17 MAP P122, B5

This brilliant repository of Arnold Schönberg's archival legacy is a cultural centre and celebration of the Viennese school of the early 20th century, honouring the Viennese-born composer, painter, teacher, theoretician and innovator known for his 12-tone technique. The exhibition hall hosts intimate classical concerts, to which in-the-know Viennese flock. (01-712 18 88; www.schoenberg.at; 03, Schwarzenbergplatz 6; 9am-5pm Mon-Fri; D Schwarzenbergplatz, U Stadtpark)

## Akademietheater

THEATRE

18 MAP P122, B4

Opened in 1922, the 500-seater Akademietheater is the second venue of Vienna's highly esteemed Burgtheater. It stages predominantly contemporary productions. (01-514 44 41 40; www.burgtheater.at; 03, Lisztstrasse 1; tickets €3.50-61; 4A Akademietheater, D, 71 Schwarzenbergplatz, U Stadtpark)

## Arena Wien

LIVE MUSIC

19 MAP P122, F6

A former slaughterhouse turned music and film venue, Arena is one of Vienna's quirkier places for seeing live acts. Hard rock, rock, metal, reggae and soul (along with cinema) fill its outdoor stage from May to September; in winter bands play in one of its two indoor halls. Regular events include the monthly German–British 1970s New Wave bash 'Iceberg'. (http://arena.wien; 03, Baumgasse 80; tickets around €15; U Erdberg, Gasometer)

## Vienna's Districts

The 23 Wiener *Bezirke* (Vienna districts) spiral out clockwise from the centre like a snail shell (but, in some instances, leapfrog position). The Innere Stadt (01) sits at the centre, encircled by the Ringstrasse. Roughly between the Ringstrasse and the Gürtel ring road are the Vorstädte (inner suburbs): 02 (Leopoldstadt), 03 (Landstrasse), 04 (Wieden), 05 (Margareten), 06 (Mariahilf), 07 (Neubau), 08 (Josefstadt) and 09 (Alsergrund). Outside the Gürtel are the Vororte (outer suburbs): 10 (Favoriten), 11 (Simmering), 12 (Meidling), 13 (Hietzing), 14 (Penzing), 15 (Rudolfsheim-Fünfhaus), 16 (Ottakring), 17 (Hernals), 18 (Währing), 19 (Döbling) and 20 (Brigittenau). Districts 21 (Floridsdorf) and 22 (Donaustadt) are on the city's northeastern flank, while 23 (Liesing) sits on the southwestern edge.

Every address in Vienna begins with the district number, starting with 01 for the Innere Stadt (inner city), with street numbers starting closest to the city. The district number is easily identifiable by the middle two digits of its four-digit post code; so, for example, 1010 is the 01 (Innere Stadt).

Each of the *Bezirke* has its own style and character. Within or straddling these districts, you'll often find smaller neighbourhoods, such as the romantic, cobblestoned Spittelberg, 07, behind the MuseumsQuartier, and the foodie favourite Freihausviertel on the edge of the 04 and 05 districts.

### Kursalon

CLASSICAL MUSIC

20 MAP P122, B3

Fans of Strauss and Mozart will love the performances at Kursalon, which holds daily evening concerts at 8.15pm devoted to the two masters of music in a splendid, refurbished Renaissance building. Also popular is the concert and dinner package (three- or four-course meal, excluding drinks, at 6pm, followed by the concert) in the equally palatial on-site restaurant. (☎01-512 57 90; www.kursalonwien.at; 01, Johannesgasse 33; tickets €45-99, concert with 3-course dinner €79-133, with 4-course dinner €84-138; 2 Weihburggasse, U Stadtpark)

Top Experience

# Run Wild at Prater

*The Prater describes two distinct areas of parkland, which comprise the city's favourite outdoor playground. First, as you enter, is the Würstelprater, with all the roller-coaster-looping, dodgem-bashing fun of the fair, where the iconic Riesenrad turns. The Unterer Prater is a vast swathe of woodland park, where Habsburgs once went hunting. Today it's perfect for gentle bike rides, walks and warm-day picnics.*

www.prater.at

admission free

U Praterstern

## Würstelprater

No matter how old you are, you're forever 10 years old with money burning a hole in your pocket at the **Würstelprater** (Prater 7; rides €1.50-5; 10am-midnight; ). Come summer, this funfair throngs with excitable tots and big kids, gorging on doughnuts and lugging around hoopla-won teddies. The fairground's 250 attractions reach from old-school ghost trains and merry-go-rounds to G-force, human-cannon-like rides.

Several white-knuckle additions to the funfair have cranked up the fear factor, including the **Turbo Boost** that spins at 100km/h; the **Ejection Seat**, a ball that dangles daredevils 90m above the ground; and the **Space Shot**, which shoots thrill-seekers like bullets at up to 80km/h. The 4km **Liliputbahn** (minirailway; www.liliputbahn.com; complete circuit adult/child €5/3; mid-Mar–late Oct; ; U Praterstern) trundles between the Würstelprater and the Ernst-Happel-Stadion.

## Riesenrad

Top of every Volksprater wishlist is the **Riesenrad** (www.wienerriesenrad.com; 02, Prater 90; adult/child €12/5; 9am-midnight, shorter hours winter; ; U Praterstern); at least for anyone of an age to recall Orson Welles' cuckoo-clock speech in British film noir *The Third Man* (1949), set in a shadowy postwar Vienna. This icon also achieved celluloid fame in the James Bond flick *The Living Daylights*, and *Before Sunrise*, directed by Richard Linklater.

Built in 1897 by Englishman Walter B Basset to celebrate the Golden Jubilee of Emperor Franz Joseph I, the Ferris wheel rises to 65m and takes about 20 minutes to rotate its 430-tonne weight one complete circle – giving you ample time to snap some fantastic shots of the city spread out at your feet. It survived bombing in 1945, and has dramatic lighting and a cafe at its base.

### ★ Top Tips

- For a truly Viennese experience, visit the farmers market at **Karmelitermarkt** (02, Karmelitermarkt; 6am-7.30pm Mon-Fri, to 5pm Sat; 2 Karmeliterplatz, U Taborstrasse), before brunch at one of the deli-cafes.

### Take a Break

Housed in an 1898 mansion, retro-grand cafe **Supersense** (https://the.supersense.com; 02, Praterstrasse 70; 2-course lunch €10, breakfast €3.80-9.20; 9.30am-7pm Tue-Fri, 10am-5pm Sat; U Praterstern) has locally roasted coffee, breakfasts and daily specials.

Intimate bistro **Tempel** (01-214 01 79; www.restaurant-tempel.at; 02, Praterstrasse 56; mains €14-24, 2-/3-course lunch €14.50/18; noon-3pm Tue-Fri, noon-3pm & 6pm-midnight Sat; U Nestroyplatz) hides in a courtyard just off Praterstrasse.

## Planetarium

The **Planetarium** (www.planetarium-wien.at; 02, Oswald-Thomas-Platz 1; adult/child €9/6.50; show times vary), Vienna's extraterrestrial and interstellar viewfinder, is located on the edge of the Würstelprater behind the Riesenrad. Shows change on a regular basis, but usually focus on how the earth fits into the cosmological scheme of things. Shows are in German.

## Pratermuseum

Sharing the same building as the Planetarium, this **municipal museum** (www.wienmuseum.at; 02, Oswald-Thomas-Platz 1; adult/under 19yr €5/free; 10am-1pm & 2-6pm Tue-Sun) traces the history of the Würstelprater and its woodland neighbour.

For all the life and splendour the Prater has seen, unfortunately its museum has only a rather dull mix of photos and stories, mainly from the 19th century. The antique slot machines, some of which are still functioning, are the museum's saving grace.

## Unterer Prater

Few places in Vienna can match the Unterer Prater for fresh air, exercise and a burst of seasonal colour. Spread across 60 sq km, central Vienna's biggest park comprises woodlands of poplar and chestnut, meadows and tree-lined boulevards, as well as children's playgrounds, a swimming pool, a golf course and a race track.

Fringed by statuesque chestnut trees that are ablaze with russet

## The Third Man

Sir Alexander Korda asked English author Graham Greene to write a film about the four-power occupation of postwar Vienna. Greene flew to Vienna in 1948 and the film, directed by Carol Reed, was shot in Vienna in the same year. It sees out-of-work writer Holly Martins (Joseph Cotton), travel to Vienna at the request of his old schoolmate Harry Lime (Orson Welles), only to find him dead under mysterious circumstances. Doubts over the death drag Martins into the black-market penicillin racket and the path of the multinational forces controlling Vienna.

*The Third Man* won first prize at Cannes in 1949 and the Academy Award for Best Cinematography (Black-and-White) in 1951, and was selected by the British Film Institute as 'favourite British film of the 20th century' in 1999. The **Burg Kino** (01-587 84 06; www.burgkino.at; 01, Opernring 19; tickets €8-9.50; D, 1, 2 Burgring, U Museumsquartier) screens the film at least three times weekly.

Its popularity has spawned the **Third Man Museum** (www.3mpc.net; 04, Pressgasse 25; adult/child €8.90/4.50, guided tour incl admission €10; 2-6pm Sat, guided tours 2pm Wed; U Kettenbrückengasse). The English-language **Third Man Tour** (www.viennawalks.com; Third Man Tour adult/child €20/17.50) covers the main filming locations, and the **3.MannTour** (01-4000 3033; www.drittemanntour.at; 01, Girardipark; tour adult/child €10/5; by reservation Thu-Sun May-Oct; U Karlsplatz) delves into Vienna's 19th-century former sewers.

RICHARD NEBESKY/LONELY PLANET ©

and gold in autumn and billowing with delicate white blossom in late spring, the **Hauptallee** avenue is the Unterer Prater's central 4.5km vein, running as straight as a die from the Praterstern to the **Lusthaus** (01-728 95 65; 02, Freudenau 254; mains €13-20; noon-10pm Mon-Tue & Thu-Fri, to 6pm Sat & Sun; ; 77A Lusthaus).

Originally erected as a 16th-century hunting lodge, the Lusthaus pavilion was rebuilt in 1783 to host imperial festivities and the like. Today, it shelters a chandelier-lit cafe and restaurant.

## Nearby: Augarten

Containing the city's oldest baroque garden, this landscaped **park** (www.kultur.park.augarten.org; 03, Obere Augartenstrasse; admission free; 6am-dusk; U Taborstrasse) from 1775 is dotted with open meadows and criss-crossed by paths lined with elm, lime, chestnut and maple trees. You can kick a ball in one section, let the kids hit the playground in another, or visit the **porcelain museum** (Augarten Porcelain Museum; www.augarten.at; 02, Obere Augartenstrasse 1; adult/child €7/5, incl guided tour €13/11; 10am-6pm Mon-Sat).

Top Experience

## Channel Mozart at Schloss Schönbrunn & Gardens

*The Habsburg empire is revealed in all its gilded glory in the wondrously ornate apartments of Schloss Schönbrunn, which are among Europe's best-preserved baroque interiors. Stories of the first public performance of Mozart or Empress Elisabeth's extreme beauty regimes bring Austrian history to life in the 40 rooms open to the public.*

01-811 13-0

www.schoenbrunn.at

13, Schönbrunner Schlossstrasse 47

8am-6.30pm Jul & Aug, to 5.30pm Apr-Jun, Sep & Oct, to 5pm Nov-Mar

U Schönbrunn, Hietzing

## Tickets for Schloss Schönbrunn

The best way to get a ticket is to buy it in advance online. Print the ticket yourself or show it on your phone to be scanned on entry.

An **Imperial Tour** ticket (adult/child €16/11.50) includes an audio-guided (or app-guided) tour of 22 rooms. A **Grand Tour** ticket (audio-guided adult/child €20/13, with guide €24/15) includes all rooms in the Imperial Tour and the additional 18 rooms of the palace that can be visited. The palace's Grand Tour accompanied by an English-speaking guide departs at 11am and 3pm daily year-round.

If you plan to see several sights at Schönbrunn, it's worth purchasing a combination ticket.

From April to October, the summer-season **Classic Pass** (adult/child €26.50/16.50) is valid for an audio-guided Grand Tour of Schloss Schönbrunn (including all 40 rooms open to the public) and visits to the Kronprinzengarten (Crown Prince Garden), Irrgarten (maze) and Labyrinth, and Gloriette with its panoramic viewing terrace. A Classic Pass that includes a guided Grand Tour per adult/child costs €30.50/18.50.

The summer-season **Classic Pass Plus** adds in the Tiergarten (zoo). With an audio-guided Grand Tour per adult/child it costs €40/23; with a guided Grand Tour it costs €44/25.

Year-round, the Sisi Ticket (p46) covering key Hofburg sites includes Schloss Schönbrunn.

## State Apartments

The Imperial Tour (using a free audio guide or app) begins at the frescoed **Blue Staircase**, which makes a regal ascent to the palace's upper level. First up are the 19th-century apartments of Emperor Franz Joseph I and his beloved wife Elisabeth, a beauty praised for her tiny waist and cascading tresses. You then visit lavishly stuccoed, chandelier-lit apartments such as the **Billiard Room**, where army officials

### ★ Top Tips

- Prepurchase tickets online to avoid queues and gain immediate entry.
- Pace yourself: this is architecture and history that overwhelms and the gardens are huge.
- To rest your feet and skip the hills, board the **Schönbrunner Panoramabahn** (www.zoovienna.at; day ticket adult/child €8/4; ⏲10am-5pm Apr-Oct) tourist 'train' (on wheels), which makes a 50-minute circuit of the grounds with nine hop-on, hop-off stops.

### Take a Break

Enjoy a drink with a spectacular view over the palace gardens to the city beyond at **Café Gloriette** (www.gloriette-cafe.at; 13, Gloriette, Schloss Schönbrunn; ⏲9am-dusk).

would pot a few balls while waiting to attend an audience, and Franz Joseph's **study**, where the emperor worked tirelessly from 5am. The iron bedstead and washstand for morning ablutions in his bedroom reveal his devout, highly disciplined nature.

Empress Elisabeth, or 'Sisi' as she is fondly nicknamed, whiled away many an hour penning poetry in the ruby-red **Stairs Cabinet**, and brushing up on various European languages while her ankle-length locks were tended in the privacy of her **dressing room**. Blue-and-white silk wall hangings adorn the **imperial bedroom** that Franz and Sisi sometimes shared. The neo-rococo **Empress' Salon** features portraits of some of Maria Theresia's 16 children, including Marie Antoinette in hunting garb, poignantly oblivious to her fate at the French guillotine in 1793.

Laid with lead crystal and fragile porcelain, the table in the **Marie Antoinette Room** is where Franz Joseph used to dig into hearty meals of goulash and schnitzel (health-conscious Sisi preferred beef broth and strawberries out of view).

More portraits of Maria Theresia's brood fill the **Children's Room** and the **Balcony Room**, graced with works by court painter Martin van Meytens. Keep an eye out for the one of ill-fated daughter **Maria Elisabeth**, considered a rare beauty before she contracted smallpox. The disease left her so disfigured that all hope of finding a husband vanished, and she entered convent life.

In the exquisite white-and-gold **Mirror Room**, a six-year-old Mozart performed for a rapturous Maria Theresia in 1762. Fairest of all is the 40m-long **Great Gallery**, where

## Schloss Schönbrunn

the Habsburgs threw balls and banquets, a frothy vision of stucco, mirrors and gilt chandeliers, topped with a fresco by Italian artist Gregorio Guglielmi showing the glorification of Maria Theresia's reign. Decor aside, this was where the historic meeting between John F Kennedy and Soviet leader Nikita Khrushchev took place in 1961.

Wandering through the porcelain-crammed **Chinese Cabinets** brings you to the equestrian fanfare of the **Carousel Room** and the **Hall of Ceremonies**, with five monumental paintings showing the marriage of Joseph, heir to the throne, to Isabella of Parma in 1760. Mozart, only four at the time of the wedding, was added as an afterthought by the artist, who took several years to complete the picture, by which time the virtuoso was a rising star.

If you have a Grand Tour ticket, you can continue through with a guide or audio guide to the palace's **east wing**. Franz Stephan's apartments begin in the sublime **Blue Chinese Salon**, where the intricate floral wall paintings are done on Chinese rice paper. The jewel-box pietra dura tables, inlaid with semiprecious stones, are stellar examples of Florentine craftsmanship. The negotiations that led to the collapse of the Austro-Hungarian Empire in 1918 were held here. A century before, Napoleon chose Schönbrunn as his HQ when he occupied Vienna in 1805 and 1809, and the **Napoleon Room** was where he may have dreamed about which country to conquer next. Look for the portrait of his only legitimate son, Napoleon II, Duke of Reichstadt, shown as a cherubic lad in the park at Schloss Laxenburg.

Passing through the exquisite rosewood **Millions Room**, the **Gobelin Salon**, filled with Flemish tapestries, and the **Red Salon** brimming with Habsburg portraits, you reach Maria Theresia's **bedroom**, with a throne-like four-poster bed covered in red velvet and gold embroidery. This is where Franz Joseph was born in 1830. Gilt-framed portraits of the Habsburgs hang on the red-damask walls of Archduke Franz Karl's **study**, and the tour concludes in the **Hunting Room**, with paintings noting Schönbrunn's origins as a hunting lodge.

## Gardens

Laid out in the formal French style, the beautifully tended palace **gardens** (admission free; ⏲6.30am-dusk), within the sprawling Schlosspark, are appealing whatever the season: a symphony of colour in the summer and a wash of greys and browns in winter. Opened to the public by Joseph II in 1779, the grounds contain a number of attractions in the tree-lined avenues that were arranged according to a grid and star-shaped system between 1750 and 1755. Between 1772 and 1780 Johann Ferdinand Hetzendorf added some of the final touches to the park under the instructions of Joseph II: fake **Roman**

**ruins** (6.30am-dusk) in 1778; the **Neptunbrunnen** (Neptune Fountain; 10am-4pm mid-Apr–Sep), an equally empire-boosting Greek-mythology-themed folly in 1781; and the crowning glory, the **Gloriette** (adult/child €4.50/3.20; 9am-7pm Jul & Aug, to 6pm Apr-Jun & Sep, to 5pm Oct-early Nov; 8A, 63A Gassmannstrasse), in 1775. The view from the Gloriette is, as the name suggests, glorious.

The palace gained its name from the **Schöner Brunnen** (10am-4pm mid-Apr–Sep). The original fountain now pours through the stone pitcher of a nymph near the Roman ruins. The garden's 630m-long **Irrgarten** (Maze; adult/child €6/3.50, combination ticket with Kindermuseum €12/8, with Kindermusum & Tiergarten €28/16; 9am-6pm mid-Mar–early Nov; ) is a classic hedge design based on the original maze that occupied its place from 1720 to 1892; adjoining this is the **Labyrinth**, a playground with games, climbing equipment and a giant mirror kaleidoscope.

East of the palace is the **Kronprinzen-garten** (Privy Garden; adult/child €3.80/3; 9am-6pm Apr-early Nov), a replica of the baroque garden that occupied the space around 1750.

## Kindermuseum

Schönbrunn's **Kindermuseum** (Children's Museum; www.kaiserkinder.at; adult/child €9.50/7.50, combination ticket with Irrgarten €12/8, with Irrgarten & Tiergarten €28/16; 10am-5pm) does what it knows best: imperialism. Activities and displays help kids discover the day-to-day life of the Habsburg court, and then dress up in princely or princessly outfits and

Palmenhaus

start ordering the serfs (parents) around. Other rooms are devoted to toys, natural science and archaeology. **Guided tours** in German are a regular feature, departing at 10.30am, 1.30pm and 3pm.

## Marionetten Theater

This small **theatre** (01-817 32 47; www.marionettentheater.at; tickets adult €11-39, child €9-25; Mon, Wed & Fri-Sun) puts on marionette performances of much-loved productions, such as *The Magic Flute* and *Aladdin* with longer performances for adults and shorter ones for families. The puppet costumes are exceptionally ornate and eye-catching. Some shows are in German and others in English.

## Wagenburg

The **Wagenburg** (Imperial Coach Collection; www.kaiserliche-wagenburg.at; adult/child €9.50/free; 9am-5pm mid-Mar–Nov, 10am-4pm Dec–mid-Mar) is *Pimp My Ride*, imperial-style. On display is a vast array of carriages, including Emperor Franz Stephan's coronation carriage, with its ornate gold plating, Venetian glass panes and painted cherubs. The whole thing weighs an astonishing four tonnes (4000kg). Also look for the dainty child's carriage built for Napoleon's son, with eagle-wing-shaped mudguards and bee motifs.

## Schönbrunn Zoo

Established in 1752 as a menagerie by Franz Stephan, the Schönbrunn **Tiergarten** (www.zoovienna.at; 13, Maxingstrasse 13b; adult/child €20/10, combination ticket with Irrgarten & Kindermuseum €28/16; 9am-6.30pm Apr-Sep, to 5.30pm Mar & Oct, to 5pm Feb, to 4.30pm Nov-Jan; 56A, 56B, 58A Tiroler Gasse) is the world's oldest continually operating zoo. Among its 8500 resident animals are giant pandas, polar bears and Siberian tigers. Feeding times are staggered throughout the day – check maps to find out who's dining when. The zoo is laid out like a bicycle wheel, with pathways as spokes and an octagonal pavilion, which dates from 1759, at its centre.

## Wüstenhaus

The small **Wüstenhaus** (Desert House; 01-877 92 94-500; www.zoovienna.at; 13, Maxingstrasse 13b; adult/child €6/4.50; 9am-6pm May-Sep, to 5pm Oct-Apr) near the Palmenhaus makes good use of the once-disused Sonnenuhrhaus (Sundial House) to re-create arid desert scenes. Its four sections – Africa, the Middle East, the Americas and Madagascar – are home to rare cacti and live desert animals.

## Palmenhaus

Londoners may think they're experiencing déjà vu on sighting the **Palmenhaus** (Palm House; 13, Maxingstrasse 13b; adult/child incl Wüstenhaus €6/4.50; 9.30am-6pm May-Sep, to 5pm Oct-Apr; U Hietzing). It was built in 1882 by Franz Segenschmid as a replica of the one in Kew Gardens. Inside is a veritable jungle of tropical plants from around the world.

SIMONE CRESPIATICO/SHUTTERSTOCK ©

# Survival Guide



Johann Strauss II statue, Rathauspark (p90) PFEIFFER/SHUTTERSTOCK ©

# Before You Go

## Book Your Stay

- Vienna has an extensive range of properties in all price categories; book ahead from Easter to September and during special events such as the Christmas markets.
- There's a smattering of *Jugendherbergen* (youth hostels), both private and hostels affiliated with Hostelling International (HI). In the former, no membership is required.
- Midrange properties span homey, often family-run *Pensionen* (guesthouses), many traditional to smart hotels and apartments.
- At the top end are luxury establishments with chandeliers, antique furniture and original 19th-century oil paintings, along with statement-making design hotels.
- Be aware that breakfast isn't always included in the overnight rate; a coffee house or cafe can often be a better-value, more atmospheric option.

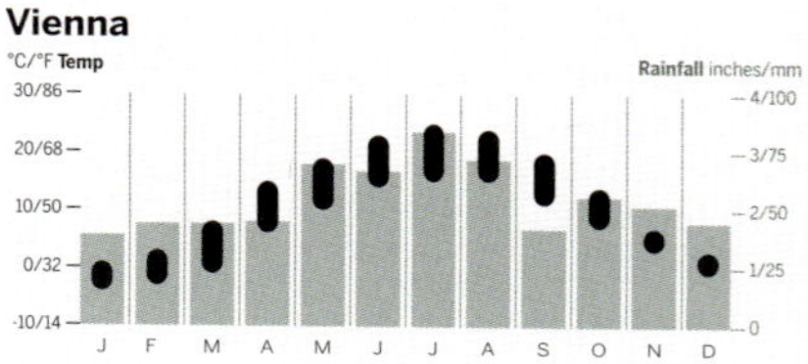


## When to Go

**Spring** (Apr–Jun) Mild temperatures, emerging greenery. Easter heralds the start of Vienna's tourist season.

**Summer** (Jul & Aug) Warm to hot weather, riverside beaches. Many restaurants, bars and smaller shops close for the *Sommerpause* (summer break).

**Autumn** (Sep & Oct) Temperatures fall, crowds tail off and Goldener Oktober brings autumnal colour.

**Winter** (Nov–Mar) Often snowy; outdoor skating rinks set up across the city.

## Useful Websites

**Lonely Planet** (lonelyplanet.com/austria/vienna/hotels) Recommendations and bookings.

**Hostelling International** (www.hihostels.com) Global youth-hostel organisation.

**Tourist Info Wien** (www.wien.info/en/hotels) Vienna's tourist office.

## Best Budget

**Grand Ferdinand Hotel** (www.grandferdinand.com) Not only sumptuous rooms and suites but mahogany bunk beds too.

**Hotel am Brillantengrund** (www.brillantengrund.com) Set around a sociable courtyard.

**my MOjO vie** (www.mymojovie.at) Hostel with bright flair.

**Wombat's City Hostel Naschmarkt** (www.wombats-hostels.com) Directly overlooking the Naschmarkt, so you can put its self-catering kitchen to use.

## Best Midrange

**Hotel Kunsthof** (www.hotelkunsthof.at) A crossover between a gallery and a hotel.

**Boutiquehotel Stadthalle** (www.hotelstadthalle.at) Cosy and eco-aware.

**Mooons** (www.mooons.com) High-tech design hotel with a great rooftop terrace.

**Hotel Capricorno** (www.schick-hotels.com/hotel-capricorno) Shimmering interiors and canal-side balconies.

## Best Top End

**Hotel Sacher** (www.sacher.com) Olde-worlde glamour and the city's most famous coffee house on the premises.

**Hotel Imperial** (www.marriott.com) Favourite for European royalty.

**Sans Souci Wien** (www.sanssouci-wien.com) Original designer furniture, pop art and a location opposite the MuseumsQuartier.

**DO & CO** (www.docohotel.com) Swanky and central, with Jacuzzis in some rooms.

# Arriving in Vienna

## Vienna International Airport

Located 19km southwest of the city centre, **Vienna International Airport** (VIE; ☎ 01-700 722 233; www.viennaairport.com; Wi-Fi) operates services worldwide. Facilities include restaurants and bars, banks and ATMs, money-exchange counters, supermarkets, a post office, car-hire agencies and two left-luggage counters open 5.30am to 11pm (per 24 hours €4 to €8; maximum six-month storage).

## Train

The **City Airport Train** (CAT; Map p102; www.cityairporttrain.com; single/return €11/19; Tram 1 Landstrasse-Wien Mitte, U Landstrasse) departs from Vienna International Airport every 30 minutes from 6.09am to 11.39pm, and from Wien-Mitte train station every 30 minutes from 5.37am to 11.07pm. Journey time is 16 minutes.

The S7 suburban train (€4.20, 37 minutes) does the same journey to/from the airport. It runs from 5.18am to 12.18am from the airport to Wien-Mitte, and from 4.19am to 11.49pm from Wien-Mitte to the airport.

## Bus

**Vienna Airport Lines** (☎ 517 17; www.viennaairportlines.at) has three services connecting different parts of Vienna to the airport. The most central is the **Vienna Airport Lines bus stop** (Map p62, C2; 01, Morzinplatz) at Morzinplatz/Schwedenplatz (bus 1185; one way/return €8/13, 20 minutes), running via the Wien-Mitte train station.

## Taxi

A taxi to/from the airport costs between €25 and €50. The yellow **Taxi 40100** (☎ 01-401 00; www.taxi40100.at) in the arrivals hall (near the bookshop) has a fixed airport rate of €36. **C&K Airport Service** (☎01-444 44; www.cundk.at) has rates starting at €33.

An Uber (www.uber.com) between the airport and city centre costs €21 to €29.

## Wien Hauptbahnhof

Vienna's main train station, the Wien Hauptbahnhof, 3km south of Stephansdom, handles all international trains as well as trains from all of Austria's provincial capitals, and many local and regional trains.

### Train

**S-Bahn** S1, S2 and S3 connect Wien Hauptbahnhof with Wien Meidling, Wien-Mitte and Praterstern.

**U-Bahn** U1 serves Karlsplatz and Stephansplatz.

### Tram

O to Praterstern, 18 to Westbahnhof and Burggasse/Stadthalle. Tram D connects Hauptbahnhof-Ost with the Ringstrasse.

### Bus

13A runs through Vienna's *Vorstädte* (inner suburbs) Margareten, Mariahilf, Neubau and Josefstadt, all between the Ringstrasse and the Gürtel.

# Getting Around

## Bicycle

- Bicycles can be carried free of charge on carriages marked with a bike symbol on the S-Bahn and U-Bahn from 9am to 3pm and after 6.30pm Monday to Friday, after 9am Saturday and all day Sunday.
- It's not possible to take bikes on trams or buses.
- The city also runs the **Citybike Wien** (Vienna City Bike; www.citybikewien.at; per 1/2/3hr free/€1/2, per hour thereafter €4) shared-bike program, with bike stands scattered throughout the city.

## Bus

Bus connections can be useful for outlying parts of town or for travellers with limited physical mobility.

### Regular Buses

Most lines run from 5am to midnight, with fewer (sometimes nonexistent) services on weekends.

**13A** Runs north–south through the Vorstädte between Hauptbahnhof and Alser Strasse.

**2A** Connects Schwarzenbergplatz, Stephansplatz, Schwedenplatz and Michaelerplatz.

**3A** Connects Börsenplatz and Schottentor with Stephansplatz and Stubentor.

### Night Buses

Nightline routes cover much of the city and run every half-hour from 12.30am to 5am.

Note that on early Saturday and Sunday mornings (ie after midnight on Fridays and Saturdays) the U-Bahn runs all night.

Schwedenplatz, Schottentor and Kärntner Ring/Oper are stopping points for many night bus services; look for buses and bus stops marked with an 'N'. All transport tickets are valid for Nightline services.

**N25** Runs around the Ringstrasse then via Schwedenplatz, Leopoldstadt to Kagraner Platz and beyond on weekdays.

## Train

### U-Bahn

- The U-Bahn (underground rail) is a quick, efficient and inexpensive way of getting around the city.
- There are five lines: U1 to U4 and U6 (there is currently no U5; construction started in 2018 and is scheduled for completion in 2023).
- Stations have lifts as well as escalators. Platforms have timetable information and signs showing the exits and nearby facilities. The U-Bahn runs from 5am to midnight Monday to Thursday and continuously from Friday through to Sunday night.

### S-Bahn

- S-Bahn trains, designated by a number preceded by an 'S', operate 10 lines from train stations and service the suburbs or satellite towns.
- Trains run from 4.30am to 1.10am.

## Tickets & Passes

Tickets and passes for **Wiener Linien** (☎01-790 91 00; www.wienerlinien.at) services (U-Bahn, trams and buses) can be purchased at U-Bahn stations and on trams and buses, in a *Tabakladen* (*Trafik;* tobacco kiosk), as well as from a few staffed ticket offices.

**Single ticket** *(Einzelfahrschein;* €2.40) Good for one journey, with line changes; costs €2.60 if purchased on trams and buses (correct change required).

**24-/48-/72-hour tickets** (€8/14.10/17.10) Require validation.

**Eight-day ticket** *(8-Tage-Klimakarte;* €40.80) Valid for eight days, not necessarily consecutive; validate the card as and when you need it.

**Weekly ticket** *(Wochenkarte;* €17.10) Valid Monday to Sunday only (ie tickets purchased on a Friday are still only valid to the Sunday).

- If you're travelling outside of Vienna, and outside of the ticket zone, you'll probably have to purchase an extension on your standard Vienna transport ticket or buy a ticket from a machine at the station; check on maps posted in train stations.

## Tram

- Vienna's tram network is extensive, with 29 lines, and it's the perfect way to view the city on the cheap.
- Trams are either numbered or lettered (eg 1, 2, D) and cover the city centre and some suburbs.
- Services run from 5.15am to 11.45pm.

## Public Transport

- Vienna's comprehensive and unified public transport network is one of the most efficient in Europe.
- Flat-fare tickets are valid for trains, trams, buses, the underground (U-Bahn) and the S-Bahn

regional trains. Services are frequent and you rarely have to wait more than 10 minutes.

- Free maps are available from **Wiener Linien** (☎01-790 91 00; www.wienerlinien.at), located in U-Bahn stations.

## Taxi

- Taxis are reliable and relatively cheap by Western European standards.
- City journeys are metered; the minimum charge is roughly €3.80 from 6am to 11pm Monday to Saturday and €4.30 any other time, plus a per-kilometre fee of €1.42.
- A telephone reservation costs an additional €2.80. A tip of 10% is expected.
- Taxis are easily found at train stations and taxi stands all over the city.
- To order one, contact **Taxi 40100** (☎01-401 00; www.taxi40100.at) They accept common credit and debit cards (check before hopping in, though).
- Uber (www.uber.com) operates in Vienna.

# Essential Information

## Accessible Travel

Vienna is becoming increasingly accessible. Ramps are common (though by no means ubiquitous). Most U-Bahn stations have wheelchair lifts. All U-Bahn stations have guiding strips for the blind. All buses these days have ramps (the driver will assist) and tilt technology, and the vast majority of the trams in service have low-floor access allowing entry in a wheelchair. Traffic lights 'bleep' to indicate when pedestrians can safely cross the road.

**Tourist Info Wien** (p151) can give advice and information. Its detailed booklet *Accessible Vienna*, in German or English, provides information on hotels and restaurants with disabled access, plus addresses of hospitals, medical-equipment shops, parking places, toilets and much more. It's available for download at www.wien.info/en/travel-info/accessible-vienna.

Download Lonely Planet's free Accessible Travel guide from http://lptravel.to/AccessibleTravel.

## Business Hours

Many restaurants, bars, entertainment venues and smaller shops shut in July and August.

**Pubs and clubs** Hours vary; generally pubs from 11am or 4pm (or 5pm), to between midnight and 4am (those serving food open earlier); clubs approximately 10pm to around 4am Thursday to Saturday.

**Restaurants** Generally 11am to 2pm and 6pm to 10pm or 11pm.

**Shops** Usually 9am to 6.30pm Monday to Friday (many to 9pm Thursday, some Friday) and until 5pm Saturday. All close Sunday.

**Supermarkets** Normally 8am to 8pm Monday to Friday, to 6pm Saturday. All close Sunday.

## Electricity

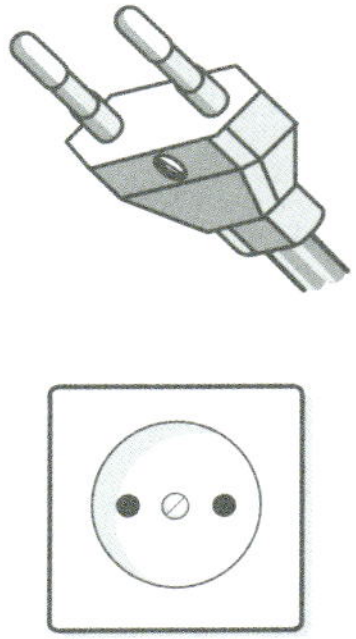

Type C
220V/50Hz

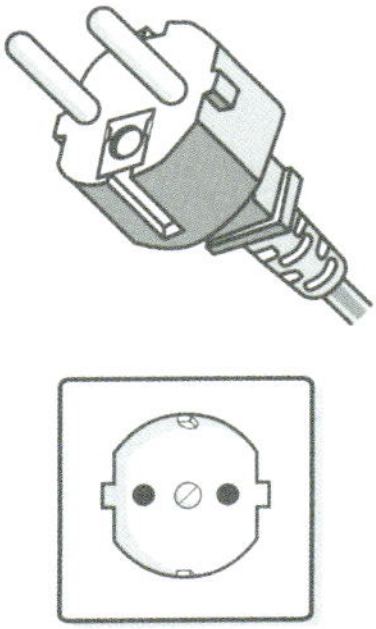

Type F
230V/50Hz

## Discount Cards

**Vienna Card** (*Die Wien-Karte;* 24/48/72 hours €17/25/29) Unlimited travel on the public-transport system (including night buses) and hundreds of discounts at selected museums, cafes, *Heurigen* (wine taverns), restaurants and shops across the city, and on guided tours and the City Airport Train. The discount is usually to 5% to 25% off the normal price. It can be bought online or at Tourist Info Wien (p151), the **Airport Information Office** (www.wien.info; 7am-10pm) and many concierge desks.

## LGBTIQ+ Travellers

Vienna is increasingly open towards LGBTIQ+ couples, more so than the rest of Austria. The country has legalised civil same-sex partnerships and marriages.

**Die Villa** (01-586 81 50; www.dievilla.at; 06, Linke Wienzeile 102; 5-8pm Mon, Wed & Fri; U Pilgramgasse), has advice and information on what's on offer in the city. The tourist office website www.wien.info/en/vienna-for/gay-lesbian has extensive information.

## Money

### ATMs

- *Bankomats* (ATMs), which accept credit cards and debit cards such as Maestro, are widespread.
- Look for a neon sign with two green and blue stripes sticking out from a bank facade.

### Credit Cards

- Visa, EuroCard and MasterCard are more widely accepted than American Express and Diners Club, although a surprising number of shops and restaurants refuse to accept any credit cards at all.
- Train tickets can be usually bought by credit card in main stations, but not all non-European cards will work – ask your bank for advice before you leave.

### Tipping

**Restaurants and cafes** Tips are generally expected; round up smaller bills (to the nearest €0.50 or euro) when buying coffee or beer, and add 5% to 10% to the bill for full meals. Tip at the time of payment as one lump sum with the bill.

**Taxis** Drivers will expect around 10% extra.

**Hotel porters and cloakroom attendants** Tip a euro or two.

## Public Holidays

The only establishments remaining open on holidays are bars, cafes and restaurants. Museums are usually open except for New Year's Day, Christmas Day and sometimes May Day. The big school break is July and August; most families go away during this time, so you'll find the city is quieter, but a high percentage of restaurants and entertainment venues close.

**New Year's Day** (Neujahr) 1 January

**Epiphany** (Heilige Drei Könige) 6 January

**Easter Monday** (Ostermontag) March or April

**Labour Day** (Tag der Arbeit) 1 May

**Ascension Day** (Christi Himmelfahrt) Sixth Thursday after Easter

**Whit Monday** (Pfingstmontag) Sixth Monday after Easter

**Corpus Christi** (Fronleichnam) Second Thursday after Pentecost

**Assumption** (Maria Himmelfahrt) 15 August

**National Day** (Nationalfeiertag) 26 October

**All Saints' Day** (Allerheiligen) 1 November

**Immaculate Conception** (Mariä Empfängnis) 8 December

**Christmas Eve** (Heiligabend) 24 December; everything closed afternoon

**Christmas Day** (Christfest) 25 December

**St Stephen's Day** (Stephanitag) 26 December

## Responsible Travel

**Overtourism**

Vienna has been one of the most active municipalities in Europe when it comes to tackling the woes of the shared economy. It's also one of the world's greenest cities. Give it a hand by avoiding Airbnb properties and other short-term rentals.Visiting Vienna in the low season (Feb-Mar and Nov) can help ease the strain.

## Safe Travel

Vienna is a very safe city and in general women and men will have no trouble walking around at night.

- Karlsplatz station and Gumpendorfer Strasse can be boisterous late in the evening.
- The Prater and Praterstern can get dodgy at night. Ausstellungsstrasse is best avoided due to sex workers and kerb-crawlers.
- The Gürtel has a sprinkling of red-light clubs: north of Westbahnhof along the Neubaugürtel has a high concentration, and directly south to Gumpendorfer Strasse can be seedy.
- S-Bahn and tram stops on Margareten and Wiedner Gürtel can be edgy.

## Telephone

**Country code** Austria's country code is 0043.

**Area code** Vienna's area code is 01. When calling from overseas drop the zero in the Vienna code.

**Prepaid SIM cards** Phone shops, kiosks and *Tabakladen* sell prepaid SIM cards. Your phone needs to be unlocked.

## Toilets

- Large shopping centres have facilities that

are free to use.

- Facilities at U-Bahn stations and public places usually incur a charge of around €0.50.
- Museums reliably have good, clean facilities.
- At cafes and bars, facilities are only for paying customers

## Dos & Don'ts

The Viennese are fairly formal and use irony to alleviate social rules and constraints.

**Greetings** *Grüss Gott* or the less formal *Servus!* are the usual forms of greeting; *Guten Tag* is also common. Stick to the polite *Sie* (you) form unless you know someone well or are of a similar age in a young-ish scene. Never use *du* with shop assistants or waiters.

**Acknowledgements** When entering a breakfast room, it's usual to acknowledge others by saying *'Guten Morgen'* when you walk in and *'Auf Wiedersehen'* on leaving.

## Tourist Information

**Tourist Info Wien** (Map p42; ☎ 01-245 55; www.wien.info; 01, Albertinaplatz; ⏰ 9am-7pm; 📶; 🚋 D, 1, 2, 71 Kärntner Ring/Oper, U Stephansplatz) Vienna's main tourist office, with a ticket agency, hotel booking service, free maps and every brochure under the sun.

**Airport Information Office** (www.wien.info; ⏰ 7am-10pm) Full services, with maps, Vienna Card and walk-in hotel booking. Located in the airport arrival hall.

**Jugendinfo** (Vienna Youth Information; Map p42; ☎ 01-4000 84 100; www.wienxtra.at/jugendinfo; 01, Babenbergerstrasse 1; ⏰ 2.30-6.30pm Mon-Fri; 🚋 D, 1, 2, 71 Burgring, U Museumsquartier) Has reduced-priced event tickets for 14 to 26 year olds. Staff have details of the city's events.

**Rathaus Information Office** (Map p62; ☎ 01-502 55; www.wien.gv.at; 01, Rathaus; ⏰ 7.30am-6pm Mon-Fri; 🚋 D, 1, 2, 71 Rathausplatz/Burgtheater, U Rathaus) The City Hall has information on social, cultural and practical matters, and is geared to residents as well as tourists.

## Visas

- Visas for stays of up to 90 days are not required for citizens of most countries, including the UK. Some nationalities, including the nationals of China, Russia and South Africa, require a visa.
- The Federal Ministry for Europe, Integration & Foreign Affairs (www.bmeia.gv.at) website has a list of Austrian embassies.
- Austria is part of the Schengen Agreement, which includes all EU states (minus the UK and Ireland) and a handful of European countries including Switzerland. In general, a visa issued by one Schengen country is good for all the other member countries.
- From 2023, non-EU nationals who don't require a visa for entry to the Schengen Area will need prior authorisation to enter under the new European Travel Information and Authorisation System (ETIAS). Travellers can apply online; the cost will be €7 for a three-year, multi-entry authorisation. Visit www.etias.com.

# Language

German is the national language of Austria. It belongs to the West Germanic language family and has around 100 million speakers worldwide.

In German, word stress falls mostly on the first syllable – in our pronunciation guides the stressed syllable is indicated with italics.

Note that German has polite and informal forms for 'you' (Sie and du respectively). When addressing people you don't know well, use the polite form. In this language guide, polite forms are used, unless you see (pol/ inf), which indicates we've given both options. Also note that (m/f) indicates masculine and feminine forms.

To enhance your trip with a phrasebook, visit lonelyplanet.com.

## Basics

**Hello.**
*Guten Tag.* goo ten tak

**Goodbye**
*Auf Wiedersehen* owf vee der zey en

**How are you?** (pol/inf)
*Wie geht es Ihnen/dir?* vee gayt es ee·nen/deer

**Fine, thanks.**
*Danke, gut.* *dang*·ke goot

**Please.**
*Bitte.* *bi*·te

**Thank you.**
*Danke.* *dang*·ke

**Excuse me./Sorry.**
*Entschuldigung.* ent·*shul*·di·gung

**Yes./No.**
*Ja./Nein.* yah/nain

**Do you speak (English)?**
*Sprechen Sie Englisch?* *shpre*·khen zee *eng*·lish

**I (don't) understand.**
*Ich verstehe (nicht).* ikh fer·*shtay*·e (nikht)

## Eating & Drinking

**I'm a vegetarian.** (m/f)
Ich bin Vegetarier/ Vegetarierin. ikh bin ve·ge·*tah*·ri·er/ ve·ge·*tah*·ri·e·in

**Cheers!**
*Prost!* prawst

**That was delicious!**
*Das war sehr lecker!* das vahr zair *le*·ker

**Please bring the bill.**
*Die Rechnung, bitte.* dee *rekh*·nung *bi*·te

**I'd like ...**
*Ich möchte ...* ikh *merkh*·te ...

| | | |
|---|---|---|
| **a coffee** | *einen Kaffee* | *ai*·nen *ka*·fay |
| **a glass of wine** | *ein Glas Wein* | ain glas wain |
| **a table for two** | *einen Tisch für zwei Personen* | *ai*·nen tish für tsvai per·*zaw*·nen |
| **two beers** | *zwei Bier* | tsvai beer |

## Shopping

**I'd like to buy ...**
*Ich möchte ... kaufen.* — ikh *merkh*·te ... *kow*·fen

**May I look at it?**
*Können Sie es mir zeigen?* — *ker*·nen zee es meer *tsai*·gen

**How much is it?**
*Wie viel kostet das?* — vee feel *kos*·tet das

**That's too expensive.**
*Das ist zu teuer.* — das ist tsoo *toy*·er

**Can you lower the price?**
*Können Sie mit dem Preis heruntergehen?* — *ker*·nen zee mit dem prais he·*run*·ter·gay·en

**There's a mistake in the bill.**
*Da ist ein Fehler in der Rechnung.* — dah ist ain *fay*·ler in dair *rekh*·nung

## Emergencies

**Help!**
*Hilfe!* — *hil*·fe

**Call a doctor!**
*Rufen Sie einen Arzt!* — *roo*·fen zee *ai*·nen artst

**Call the police!**
*Rufen Sie die Polizei!* — *roo*·fen zee dee po·li·*tsai*

**I'm lost.**
*Ich habe mich verirrt.* — ikh *hah*·be mikh fer·*irt*

**I'm ill.**
*Ich bin krank.* — ikh bin krangk

**Where's the toilet?**
*Wo ist die Toilette?* — vo ist dee to·a·*le*·te

## Time & Numbers

**What time is it?**
*Wie spät ist es?* — vee shpayt ist es

**It's (10) o'clock.**
*Es ist (zehn) Uhr.* — es ist (tsayn) oor

| | | |
|---|---|---|
| **morning** | *Morgen* | *mor*·gen |
| **afternoon** | *Nachmittag* | *nahkh*·mi·tahk |
| **evening** | *Abend* | *ah*·bent |
| **yesterday** | *gestern* | *ges*·tern |
| **today** | *heute* | *hoy*·te |
| **tomorrow** | *morgen* | *mor*·gen |

| | | |
|---|---|---|
| **1** | *eins* | ains |
| **2** | *zwei* | tsvai |
| **3** | *drei* | drai |
| **4** | *vier* | feer |
| **5** | *fünf* | fünf |
| **6** | *sechs* | zeks |
| **7** | *sieben* | zee·ben |
| **8** | *acht* | akht |
| **9** | *neun* | noyn |
| **10** | *zehn* | tsayn |
| **100** | *hundert* | *hun*·dert |
| **1000** | *tausend* | *tow*·sent |

## Transport & Directions

**Where's ...?**
*Wo ist ...?* — vaw ist ...

**What's the address?**
*Wie ist die Adresse?* — vee ist dee a·dre·se

**Can you show me (on the map)?**
*Können Sie es mir (auf der Karte) zeigen?* — *ker*·nen zee es meer (owf dair *kar*·te) *tsai*·gen

**I want to go to ...**
*Ich mochte nach ... fahren.* — ikh *merkh*·te nahkh ... *fah*·ren

**What time does it leave?**
*Wann fährt es ab?* — van fairt es ap

**What time does it arrive?**
*Wann kommt es an?* — van komt es an

**Does it stop at ...?**
*Hält es in ...?* — helt es in ...

**I want to get off here.**
*Ich mochte hier aussteigen.* — ikh *merkh*·te heer ows·shtai·gen

# Behind the Scenes

## Send Us Your Feedback

We love to hear from travellers – your comments help make our books better. We read every word, and we guarantee that your feedback goes straight to the authors. Visit **lonelyplanet.com/contact** to submit your updates and suggestions. Note: We may edit, reproduce and incorporate your comments in Lonely Planet products such as guidebooks, websites and digital products, so let us know if you don't want your comments reproduced or your name acknowledged. For a copy of our privacy policy visit lonelyplanet.com/legal.


## Catherine's Thanks

*Vielen Dank* to Julian, as well as all the locals and fellow travellers in Vienna for insights during this update and over the years. Huge thanks, too, to my Vienna co-author Kerry and to Brana Vladisavljevic, Dan Fahey, and all at LP. *Merci encore* to my parents, brother, *belle-sœur*, *neveu* and *nièce*.

## Kerry's Thanks

A big thank you goes out to all the people I met on my travels, including tourism professionals Bettina Jamy-Stowasser and Helena Hartlauer in Vienna. Special thanks, too, to Eugene Quinn at Space and Place in Vienna.

## Acknowledgements

Cover photograph: Graben; Hiroshi Higuchi/Getty Images © Back cover photograph: Pastries, Christmas market; anzeletti/Getty Images ©. Photographs on pp32-3 (clockwise from left): Tmp_an_instant_of_time/Shutterstock, Bluejayphoto/Getty Images, Vvoe/Shutterstock, Gregor Schuster/Getty Images ©

## This Book

This 4th edition of Lonely Planet's *Pocket Vienna* guidebook was curated by Catherine Le Nevez and researched and written by Catherine, Kerry Walker and Marc di Duca. The previous two editions were also written by Catherine. This guidebook was produced by the following:

**Commissioning Editor** Daniel Bolger

**Senior Product Editors** Genna Patterson, Sandie Kestell, Kathryn Rowan

**Product Editor** Gary Quinn

**Book Designer** Katherine Marsh

**Assisting Editors** Nigel Chin, Andrea Dobbin, Trent Holden, Jodie Martire, Rosie Nicholson, Lauren O'Connell, Kristin Odijk, Mani Ramaswamy, Fionnuala Twomey, Maja Vatrić

**Cartographers** Julie Dodkins, Mark Griffiths

**Cover Researcher** Meri Blazevski

**Thanks to** Ronan Abayawickrema, Ross Estes Blum, Mark Duncan, Catherine Farren, Shona Gray, Sonia Kapoor Catherine Naghten, David Shade, Angela Tinson

# Index

See also separate subindexes for:

Eating p157
Drinking p157
Entertainment p158
Shopping p158



**Sights 000**
Map Pages **000**

**Sights 000**
Map Pages **000**

## Entertainment



## Shopping



**Sights 000**
Map Pages **000**